JUNIOR NATURE GUIDE
WILD FLOWERS

Written by Angela Royston

www.alligatorbooks.co.uk

Countryside Code

1 Always go out with a friend, and always tell an adult where you are going.
2 Only pick a flower growing in the wild if you are sure it is common.
3 Only pick one or two flowers and then only from a large clump.
4 Leave the roots behind of flowers you pick and don't dig up bulbs or plants to take home.
5 Keep to footpaths as much as possible, and don't walk on wild flowers.
6 Keep off crops and leave fence gates as you find them.
7 Ask permission before exploring or crossing private property.
8 Take your litter home.

ISBN-13: 978-1-84239-948-4
ISBN-10: 1-84239-948-9

© 2006 Alligator Books Limited
Published by Alligator Books Limited
Gadd House, Arcadia Avenue,
London N3 2JU

Printed in Malaysia

Contents

Introduction...................... 4–5
What to look for................ 6–7

**Cultivated & Waste
Land**.............................. 8–21
Green Flowers................ 10–11
Yellow Flowers................ 12–15
White Flowers................ 16–17
Pink Flowers.................... 18–19
Blue & Purple Flowers....... 20–21
How Plants Make Seeds... 22–23

Roadsides & Hedges...... **24–25**
Yellow & White Flowers.... 26–27
White Flowers................ 28–31
Pink & Purple Flowers....... 32–33
Blue & Violet Flowers........ 34–35
Growing Your Own.......... 36–37

Woodlands...................... **38–47**
Green Flowers................ 40–41
Yellow & White Flowers.... 42–43
White Flowers................ 44–45
Red, Blue & Purple Flowers 46–47
Experiments with Plants 48–49

Meadows & Pastures...... **50–59**
Green & White Flowers..... 52–53
Yellow Flowers................ 54–55
Pink Flowers.................... 56–57
Blue & Purple Flowers....... 58–59
Preserving Wild Flowers 60–61

Rivers, Lakes & Ponds.... **62–69**
White Flowers................ 63–65
Yellow Flowers................ 66–67
Pink, Brown & Purple Flowers
..................................68–69
Things to Make.............. 70–71

Seashores...................... **72–77**
Yellow Flowers...................... 73
Green Flowers................ 74–75
White & Pink Flowers........ 76–77

Find Out Some More........... 78
Index.............................. 79–80

Introduction

There are thousands of different wild flowers in Great Britain and Europe. Not only are they beautiful, but many are useful, too. You might be surprised at how many plants have been used as herbal medicines for hundreds of years.

Lots of wild plants used to be eaten raw or cooked, but others are extremely poisonous. Only eat plants that you have grown specially in your own garden, and make sure the seed packet says it is for eating – always ask an adult first!

Being able to identify wild flowers is useful as well as fun. But, with so many different flowers that you might find, where do you start?

This book has been planned to help you in two ways. It shows only the flowers you are most likely to see and it groups them according to the habitat, or type of countryside, where you are most likely to see them. There are six main habitats described in this book, ranging from the city to the seashore.

The life of a plant

Look for plants at all stages of their life cycle, as buds, fruits and flowers. Dandelions are perennial plants. They can live for several [or many] years and produce flowers and seeds every year. Many perennials grow from bulbs or from thick underground roots or stems that store up food to last the plants through the winter.

Biennial plants live for just two growing seasons, while annual plants complete their lives in just one growing season.

To find out more about how plants produce seeds, look at pages 22–23.

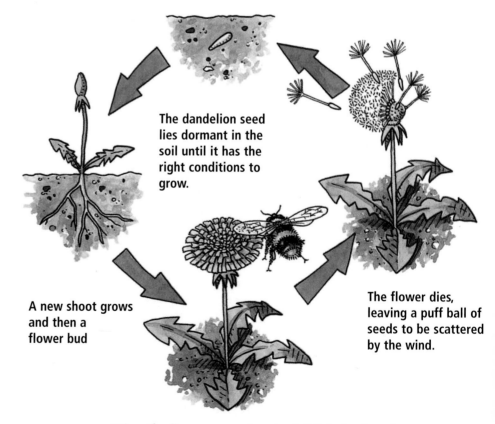

The dandelion seed lies dormant in the soil until it has the right conditions to grow.

A new shoot grows and then a flower bud

The flower dies, leaving a puff ball of seeds to be scattered by the wind.

When the flower opens, insects visit it to feed on the pollen and nectar.

How to use this book

To identify a flower you do not recognize – for example, the pink and the white flowers shown here – follow these steps.

1 **Decide what habitat you are in.** The descriptions at the start of each section will help. Each habitat has a different picture band.

2 **What colour is your flower?** Look at the pages of flowers with this colour and picture band. The picture and information given for each flower will help you identify it. The pink flower is Field Bindweed (on page 18).

3 **If you can't find the flower**, look for it under another colour. Some flowers vary in colour. White clover, for example, can have white or pink flowers.

4 **If you can't find the flower in that section**, look through other habitats for flowers of that colour. Some flowers grow in more than one kind of habitat. The white flower is Wild Carrot (on page 53).

5 **If you still can't find the flower**, you may have to look in a larger field guide (see page 78 for some suggestions). You may have found something that is very rare!

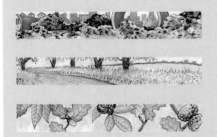

Habitat Picture Bands

Each habitat has a different picture band at the top of the page. These are shown below.

Cultivated and Waste Land	Meadows and Pastures
Roadsides and Hedges	Rivers, Lakes and Ponds
Woodlands	Seaside

What To Look For

Parts of a flower

The shapes of flowers and the colour of their petals may be very different from one kind of plant to another, but all flowers have the same parts and fulfil the same purpose. They make seeds so that the plant can reproduce itself. To do this the male pollen has to fertilize the female ovules.

Members of the daisy family, among others, have lots of tiny flowers packed into one composite flowerhead.

These strap-like petals are really tiny flowers called ray florets.

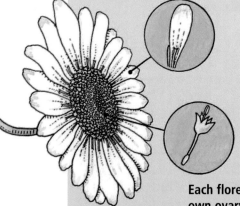

Each floret has its own ovary.

The centre of this daisy is made up of tiny flowers called disk florets.

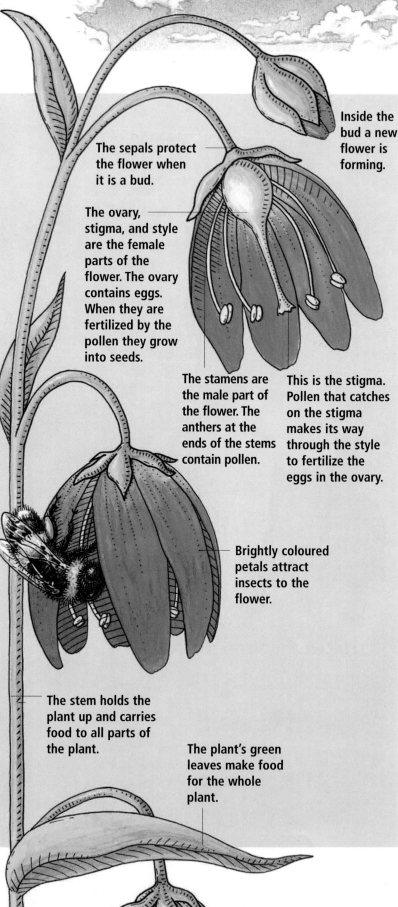

The sepals protect the flower when it is a bud.

Inside the bud a new flower is forming.

The ovary, stigma, and style are the female parts of the flower. The ovary contains eggs. When they are fertilized by the pollen they grow into seeds.

The stamens are the male part of the flower. The anthers at the ends of the stems contain pollen.

This is the stigma. Pollen that catches on the stigma makes its way through the style to fertilize the eggs in the ovary.

Brightly coloured petals attract insects to the flower.

The stem holds the plant up and carries food to all parts of the plant.

The plant's green leaves make food for the whole plant.

Arrangement of flowers

Some plants have a single flower, others have clusters of flowers. Look for the particular shapes of clusters.

Umbel   Domed   Composite   Cluster   Spike

Shapes of leaves

Always check the shape of the leaves of a plant. They are sometimes the only way to tell one plant from another that is like it.

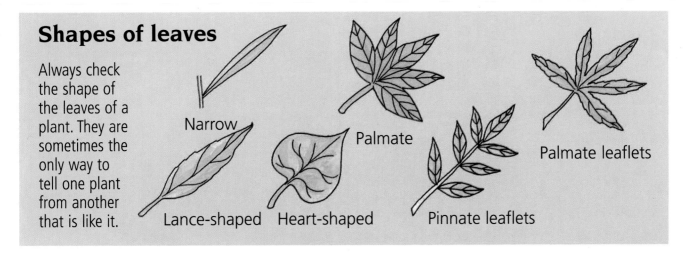

Narrow

Palmate

Palmate leaflets

Lance-shaped   Heart-shaped   Pinnate leaflets

How leaves grow

Leaves grow in different ways up the stem. Look for these arrangements.

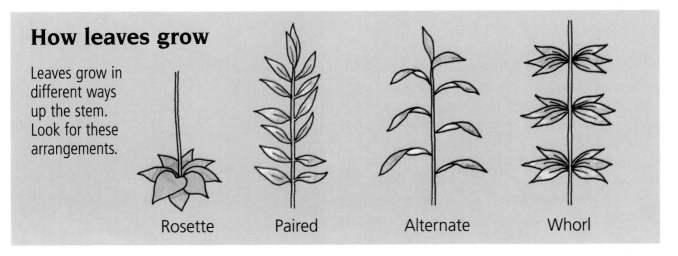

Rosette   Paired   Alternate   Whorl

Cultivated & Waste Land

Cultivated land includes vegetable plots in gardens and allotments, as well as ploughed fields. Cultivated and waste land provide similar chances for plants – a wide expanse of bare soil just waiting for seeds to grow in it. Seeds are carried here by the wind, or on people's clothes or animal fur.

Plants that thrive here include Chickweed, Groundsel and Scarlet Pimpernel. They grow fast, and produce flowers and seeds in a short time. They can withstand the wind and sun but do not like competing for space, water or light. As other plants grow they die back, but already their seeds have been scattered to new ground, or lie dormant in the soil until it is dug over or ploughed again.

You can find small patches of waste ground almost anywhere in cities and countryside. Large patches vary from railway sidings to abandoned factory sites. You are sure to find Nettles and Docks, but look too for more exotic plants, those whose seeds have escaped from gardens, or foreign plants such as Policeman's Helmet and Evening Primrose. At some time their seeds came to this country by accident, brought in on people's clothes, among other seeds, or with timber.

There is no shortage of arable land, but sadly fewer and fewer wild flowers grow there now. More efficient methods of cleaning seeds and killing weeds mean that Ox-eye Daisies, Poppies, Corn Cockles and other colourful weeds are disappearing from our fields. Look for them on roadsides instead. The picture shows seven plants from this book; how many can you recognize?

Field Bindweed, Burdock, Red Deadnettle, Dock, Groundsel, Smooth Hawk's-beard, Creeping Thistle

Common Orache

Orache looks rather like Good King Henry but if you look closely you will see that its narrow, arrow-shaped leaves are more or less covered with white hairs. Its spikes of greenish flowers each grow from the base of a narrow leaf. Orache leaves are rich in Vitamin C and taste good when cooked.

Goosefoot family
Up to 1.5 m tall
Flowers from July to September
Often grows near the sea

Greater Plantain

Look for this plant on well-trodden ground. It grows from a flat rosette of broad oval leaves. Notice their ridged veins and long stalks. The small green flowers form long spikes. Look for the purple stamens sticking out beyond the flowers. The young leaves of many plantains can be cooked as a vegetable and the seeds can be ground into flour.

Plantain family
Up to 60 cm tall
Flowers from June to September
Also grows on roadsides, lawns and footpaths

Stinging Nettle

Nettles are easy to spot by their tall upright stems and toothed leaves. But be careful, both the leaves and stems are covered with fine hairs which will sting you if you brush against them, and leave you with a burning red rash on your skin. In summer look for the tiny green flowers growing in drooping clusters at the base of each leaf stalk. Nettle leaves can be cooked and eaten as a vegetable.

Nettle family
1–1.2 m tall
Flowers from June to August
Also grows in hedgerows, woods and on roadsides

Curled Dock

These long leaves with their curly edges are easy to spot. They are very common and often grow near Stinging Nettles. Rubbing one on a nettle sting is an old and useful remedy. The small, greenish flowers grow in whorls up the flowering stem. Look out for the red fruits which are surrounded by three green 'wings'.

Dock family
Up to 1 m tall
Flowers from June to September
Also grows on roadsides

Sun Spurge

Sun Spurge grows from a single stem with oval shaped, finely toothed leaves. The stem branches near the top into umbels of flowers. Look closely at one of the flowerheads and you will see the single green female flower in the centre surrounded by male flowers. Notice the leafy bracts which cup the flowerheads. Handle spurges carefully – they have burning, milky sap.

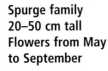

Spurge family
20–50 cm tall
Flowers from May to September

Good King Henry

Look for the many short spikes of small, greenish flowers. They grow at the top of the stem and from the base of the leaves. The leaves are triangular, rarely with any teeth, and grow up to 10 cm long. When they are young the leaves look mealy underneath, as if sprinkled with flour. Then they can be eaten in salads, and the shoots can be cooked and eaten like asparagus.

Goosefoot family
Up to 60 cm tall
Flowers from May to July
Also grows on roadsides

Rough Cocklebur

You are most likely to see this strange plant growing on rubbish tips in south-east England. It is a rough-looking plant with branched stems and rounded triangular leaves. The flowers grow in rounded heads at the base of the leaves. Look out for the fruits. They are about 2 cm long with slender spines, which catch in your clothes or on animals' fur.

Daisy family
20–120 cm tall
Flowers from June to September

Hedge Mustard

Hedge Mustard forms long flowering stems which soon turn into rows of overlapping seed pods with small clusters of pale yellow flowers at the tops. Notice how the seed pods are pressed close against the stem, and how the flowering stems themselves jut out from the main stem, almost at right angles. The leaves round the base are deeply cut, but those on the stem are narrow and toothed.

Mustard family
About 60 cm tall
Flowers from June to July
Also grows on hedgebanks and roadsides

Wild Radish

Wild Radish is also known as White Charlock and is similar to Charlock. Its leaves, however, are heavily lobed near the stem and its yellow flowers become white as they age. Notice that the petals have mauve veins. Look out for the long seed pods. They point upwards and, as they dry out, they shrink around each seed so you can clearly see the seed's shape.

Mustard family
20–60 cm tall
Flowers June to September

Treacle Mustard

You are most likely to see this plant in southern England. Look for the flat-topped clusters of bright yellow flowers. Look too for the long, curved seed pods growing on the stem below them. The pods get longer the lower down the stem they are. Another name for the plant is Wormseed because its seeds were once used as a remedy for worms. But do not try it. Too large a dose can be dangerous.

Mustard family
Up to 90 cm tall
Flowers from June to August
Also grows on roadsides

Charlock

These plants with their bright yellow flowers, are also called Wild Mustard. The flowers grow on upright stems covered with stiff hairs, the lower ones opening first. You will see their long, beaked seed pods while the upper flowers are still in bloom. The plant produces so many seeds it used to be a serious nuisance to farmers, sometimes taking over whole fields from crops. Now it is controlled with weed-killers.

Mustard family
30–90 cm tall
Flowers from May to July
Also grows on roadsides

Field Pansy

Look for this plant with its small, creamy-coloured flowers sprawling over the ground in waste places as well as fields. The petals are often tinged with yellow or blue. The flowers grow on long stalks from a whorl of leaves. The leaves are lance shaped and some are so divided that they are almost pinnate.

Violet family
Up to 30 cm tall
Flowers April to September

Common Evening Primrose

These yellow, scented flowers open a few at a time and only in the evening. Each flower has four showy petals and several long stamens. The leaves are lance shaped and grow alternately up the stem. The flowers are followed by large, oblong capsules which point more or less upright. Evening Primrose oil comes from the plant. It soothes inflamed skin, eases coughs and helps to prevent heart disease.

Willowherb family
Up to
1.5 m tall
Flowers
from
July to
September

Ribbed Melilot

Like Dyer's Rocket, this is a tall plant with a slender spike of yellow flowers. However, the flowers are totally different in shape, being like pea-flowers. Ribbed Melilot has three leaflets, rather like those of clover. As the flowers and plants dry, they smell of new-mown hay. Then they give way to brown seed pods. This plant is common only in eastern Ireland and England.

Pea family
Up to 1.5 m tall
Flowers from July to September
Also grows on roadsides

Dyer's Rocket

Look for the long slender spike of yellow-green flowers growing at the top of this tall plant. The leaves are narrow with wavy edges and grow alternately up the stem. The plant is also called Weld, but the name Dyer's Rocket is a reminder that for hundreds of years it was grown commercially to produce a bright yellow dye, which has now been replaced by synthetic dye.

Mignonette family
Up to 1.5 m tall
Flowers from June to August
Also grows on roadsides and sand dunes

Coltsfoot

Look for the flowers of Coltsfoot early in the year. The yellow flowerheads look rather like dandelions, but grow at the end of scaly red stems. They are followed by 'clocks' of white-haired seeds. The leaves appear last of all and cover the ground in summer. At first they are covered with white hairs but soon become deep green on top. Coltsfoot is used in both herbal and commercial cough remedies.

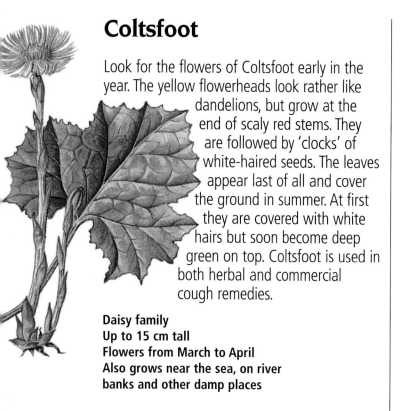

Daisy family
Up to 15 cm tall
Flowers from March to April
Also grows near the sea, on river banks and other damp places

Garden Parsley

This is the same plant that grows in your garden as a kitchen herb. But do not eat wild plants because it is easy to confuse it with Fool's Parsley which is very poisonous (see page 17). The leaves are divided into a series of three leaflets, each crisply curled round the edges. They smell clearly of parsley. Look for the flat-topped umbels of yellowish flowers around mid-summer.

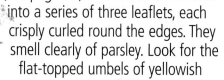

Carrot family
Up to 75 cm tall
Flowers from June to August

Smooth Hawksbeard

At first glance the flowers of this plant look like many small dandelions. The leaves at the stem base are like dandelion leaves too, but higher up they are smaller and simpler. One or more branching stems grow from the same clump of leaves. The flowers give way to parachuted seed heads, each with many rows of soft white hairs.

Daisy family
Up to 90 cm tall
Flowers from June to September
Also grows on roadsides, walls and heaths

Dandelion

Dandelions are one of the best-known flowers. Look for the rosette of wavy, lobed leaves. The stalks are hollow and they and the leaves ooze a milky juice if broken. The flowerheads are followed by 'clocks' of parachuted seeds which are blown in the wind. The leaves can be eaten in salads and the roots can be roasted and ground to make a substitute for coffee.

Daisy family
Up to 30 cm tall
Flowers April to August
Grows on waste ground, lawns and other grassy places

Prickly Sow-thistle

This plant looks like a cross between a dandelion and a thistle. The leaves are very prickly. Notice how the bases of the lower ones clasp the stem. The yellow flowerheads grow at the end of the stems and there may be few or many of them.

Daisy family
Up to 1.5 m tall
Flowers from June to August
Also grows on
roadsides

Nipplewort

Look for the small, yellow flowerheads of this plant growing on many thin branches at the top of the tall stems. The leaves near the top of the stem are lance shaped, but those lower down have several small lobes, or wings, near the base. The young leaves can be eaten raw in salads or cooked like spinach.

Daisy family
Up to 120cm tall
Flowers from July
to September
Also grows on roadsides
and in hedgerows

Groundsel

The flowers of Groundsel are like the yellow centres of daisies surrounded by a cup of green bracts tipped with black. They look like small old-fashioned shaving brushes. The leaves are toothed and ragged. The flowers give way to a ball of white hairs which carry the seeds away in the wind. The plant is so successful it can take over large areas if left to do so.

Daisy family
Up to 30 cm tall
Flowers from February to November
Also grows on roadsides

Prickly Lettuce

The pale yellow flowerheads of this plant grow on many short branches at the top of the tall stems. They are followed by clusters of parachuted seeds. The stem is covered with leaves which have prickly edges and prickly veins underneath. The plant is sometimes called Compass Plant, because when it grows in full sunlight the leaves grow upright and point east and west.

Daisy family
Up to 2 m tall
Flowers from July to September
Also grows on sand dunes

Cultivated & Waste Land

Field Pennycress

The most noticeable things about Field Pennycress are its rotten smell, and its seeds, which give the plant its name. The long spike of small white flowers gradually gives way to round flattened fruits. Each has two wings and is said to look like an old penny. The leaves are toothed and lance shaped and grow alternately up the stem.

Mustard family
Up to 60 cm tall
Flowers from May to July

Corn Spurrey

This plant is easy to spot with its long, slender, green stem and whorls of long narrow leaves. The small white flowers grow in clusters at the end of the stems. If you look carefully at one you will see that each has five petals with green sepals between them. Feel the stem too. It is covered with small, sticky hairs.

Pink family
Up to 40 cm tall
Flowers from June to August
Also grows on roadsides

Scentless Mayweed

This plant is one of several that look like large daisies, but unlike many of the others it has no scent. Each sprawling stem has several flowerheads and its leaves are divided into many narrow segments. As the summer wears on, the flowerheads begin to age and droop. Notice how the white outer florets bend down to the stalk.

Daisy family
Up to 60 cm tall
Flowers from July to September

Hoary Cress

You will probably see this plant in a large spreading patch. It has deep roots and spreads quickly where it takes hold. Its thick clusters of white flowers are hard to miss, but look too at the leaves. They are deeply toothed and generally hairless, or sparsely hairy. The fruits are kidney shaped but split into single seeds on the flower stalks.

Mustard family
Up to 90 cm tall
Flowers from May to June
Also grows on roadsides

Shepherd's Purse

This common weed is found throughout the world. Like Field Pennycress, it is called after its seeds. The tiny white flowers give way to heart shaped capsules, which look like little purses. The plant grows from a rosette of leaves. They are lance shaped and deeply lobed. A few leaves also grow up the stem.

Mustard family
Up to 40 cm tall
Flowers all year round

Common Chickweed

Chickweed plants have weak stems and many oval leaves. Look for the tiny white flowers growing between the leaves at the ends of the stems. Look too for the single line of hairs that runs down the stem. Chickweed can be eaten in salads, but it tastes so bitter it is better boiled as a vegetable.

Pink family
Up to 40 cm tall
Flowers from March to October
Also found in woods and gardens

Fool's Parsley

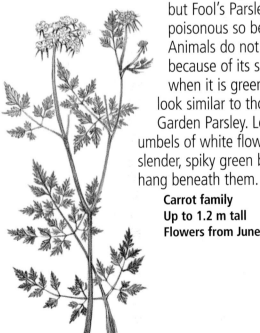

This plant can be easily mistaken for Garden Parsley (see page 14), but Fool's Parsley is very poisonous so be careful. Animals do not eat it because of its stinking smell when it is green. The leaves look similar to those of Garden Parsley. Look for the umbels of white flowers and the slender, spiky green bracts which hang beneath them.

Carrot family
Up to 1.2 m tall
Flowers from June to August

Ground Elder

Look for the thick, rounded umbels of white flowers in summer. Each flowerhead has 10–20 rays. The leaves are pinnate and cover the ground in spring. Another name for Ground Elder is Goutweed, because at one time it was used as a herbal remedy for gout and rheumatism. It was also grown in gardens for its leaves, which can be cooked and eaten like spinach.

Carrot family
30–100 cm tall
Flowers from June to July
Often found in old gardens

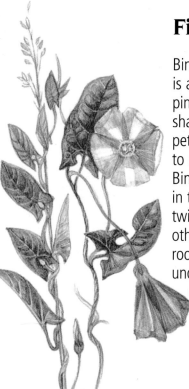

Field Bindweed

Bindweed is easy to recognize. It is a creeping or climbing vine with pink or white flowers and arrow-shaped leaves. Notice how the five petals of each flower join together to make a funnel. Look for Field Bindweed straggling over fences in tangles of climbing stems, or twisting anticlockwise around other plants. You won't see the roots, as they go deep underground, up to 2 m or more.

Bindweed family
30–75 cm tall
Flowers from June to September
Also grows on roadsides

Red Deadnettle

The leaves of this plant look like those of Stinging Nettles (see page 10), but they will not sting you. To tell the plants apart, look at the flowers. Those of Red Deadnettle are pinkish-purple and grow in thick whorls at the tops of the stems. The plant was used as an old herbal remedy for diarrhoea and to stop bleeding.

Mint family
Up to 45 cm tall
Flowers from March to September

Knotgrass

Although Knotgrass has long stems, they sprawl along the ground. Look for the small, pinkish flowers between the base of the leaves and the stem. The leaves are narrow and lance shaped. They get smaller the farther along the stems they are. The brown fruits can last in the soil for many years, and so seem to spring up like magic on newly disturbed ground.

Dock family
Stems up to 2 m long
Flowers from July to October
Also grows on seashores

Cut-leaved Crane's-bill

Crane's-bills are the wild members of the geranium family. The pot-plant geraniums come mainly from hot countries. The small reddish-pink flowers of Cut-leaved Crane's-bill grow in clusters at the end of the straggling stems. Look for its leaves which, as its name suggests, are deeply divided almost to their base.

Geranium family
Stems up to 60 cm long
Flowers from May to August
Also found in hedgerows and on roadsides

Rosebay Willowherb

This plant is easy to spot. It forms large colonies with bright red-purple flowers in long spikes opening from the bottom first. The plant is even more noticeable when it is in seed. The seed capsules are 7 cm long and they open to reveal long silky hairs which carry the seeds away in the wind.

Willowherb family
Up to 2 m tall
Flowers from
July to September
Also grows on
roadsides,
riverbanks and
in woods

Field Poppy

You cannot miss the bright-red flowers of this plant. It is well known as the symbol of Remembrance Day. The four petals open from nodding buds and surround the black anthers in the centre of the flower. Look out for the pepperpot of seeds which follows the flower. It has a row of small holes around the rim. When the wind blows, the many seeds inside are shaken out of the holes and scattered.

Poppy family
Up to 60 cm tall
Flowers from June to August
Also found on roadsides

Scarlet Pimpernel

You will only see the attractive red flowers of this plant fully open on bright sunny mornings. They close at about 3.00 pm and stay closed in dull weather. This has led to its many folk names, such as Shepherd's Clock and Poor Man's Weatherglass. Look for the sprawling stems and pointed oval leaves growing in pairs. Look too for the seed capsules; they have hinged lids that open to release the seeds.

Primrose family
Low-growing
Flowers from June to August
Also grows on roadsides,
sand dunes and in gardens

Field Forget-me-not

Look for the bright-blue flowers of this plant growing in clusters at the end of their stems. The clusters are coiled at first and only unfurl as the flowers gradually open. Each flower is tiny – about 3 mm across. Look for the oval leaves, which grow alternately up the stem. Look too for the rosette of leaves at the bottom of the stem.

Forget-me-not family
Up to 30 cm tall
Flowers from April to August
Also grows on roadsides and sand dunes

Common Fumitory

You can recognize Fumitory from its strange flowers. They grow in loose spikes and each one makes a pink tube with red tips. Each flower appears to be balanced on its stalk. The leaves are deeply divided. Fumitory comes from the Latin word for smoke, and the plant gets its name from the way its blue-green leaves spread across the ground.

Fumitory family
Up to 30 cm tall
Flowers from June to September

Creeping Thistle

Most thistles have prickly stems, prickly leaves, and prickly bracts around the base of the flowerhead. Creeping Thistle has spiny leaves, but smooth stems. Its pale purple flowerheads grow alone or in clusters among the upper leaves. The flowers are followed by many fluffy brown balls of seeds which blow away in the wind. The plant itself, however, spreads far and wide by means of its long creeping roots.

Daisy family
Up to 1.5 m tall
Flowers from July to September
Also grows on roadsides and paths, and in pastures and woods

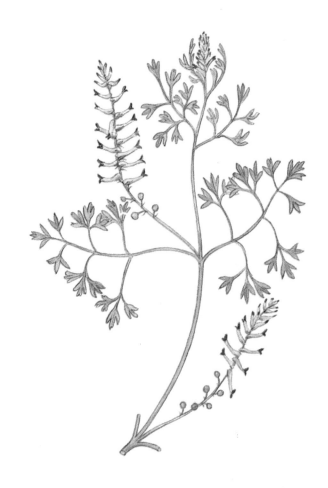

Lesser Burdock

The red-purple flowers of this plant peer out of the top of their swollen bases. Look for the hooked bracts which cover the base. The flowers are followed by hooked 'burrs' which cling to animals' fur and perhaps to your own clothing. Look too at the leaves. They have long stalks and are rather heart shaped, particularly lower down the stem. The young leaves are rich in Vitamin C and can be eaten.

Daisy family
About 1.2 m tall
Flowers from July to September
Also found on roadsides and in open woods

Selfheal

As its name shows, this plant was once used to help wounds heal, but it is not much used today. Look for the blue-violet flowers, which grow in thick clusters at the tops of the stems. They each have two lips and many hairy bracts. The leaves are oval or lance shaped and are sometimes toothed. They grow in pairs on short stalks.

Mint family
Up to 50 cm tall
Flowers from July to September
Also grows in grassy places, roadsides and woods

Ivy-leaved Speedwell

You are most likely to see this plant as a thick sprawling mat of stems and leaves. The light-green leaves are rather thick and palmate. They look similar to ivy leaves, as the name suggests. The pale blue or lilac flowers grow on long stalks from the base of the end leaves.

Figwort family
Stems up to 60 cm long
Flowers from April to May

How Plants Make Seeds

Plants produce eggs (known as ovules) in the female part of the flower (the ovary) and pollen grains in the male part of the flower (the anthers). If you don't know where these bits of the flower are, look at pages 6 and 7, which tell you 'what to look for'. Pollen grains are carried from one flower to another by the wind or by animals, usually insects.

Stigma — Pollen

Anthers

Style

— Ovules

Ovary

Insects are attracted to flowers by their bright petals, their scent and their sweet-tasting nectar. As they feed on the nectar and pollen, some pollen sticks to their bodies and is rubbed off on the next flower they visit.

If it is pollen from the same kind of flower and it sticks to the stigma, the pollen grain sends a tube down the style and into the ovary. There the contents of the pollen grain join with an ovule to fertilize it so that it starts to grow into a seed.

When most of the ovules have been fertilized, the petals begin to wither and die. The seeds swell and grow in the ovary until they are ready to be scattered.

Pollinating a tomato plant

Only the right sort of pollen will fertilize the ovules. In this experiment you are the pollinator. You will take the pollen from one flower to another.

1 **Buy one or two tomato plants** and plant them in pots of compost. Use large pots, because they will grow up to 1.5 m tall. Put them in a sunny place and water them regularly.

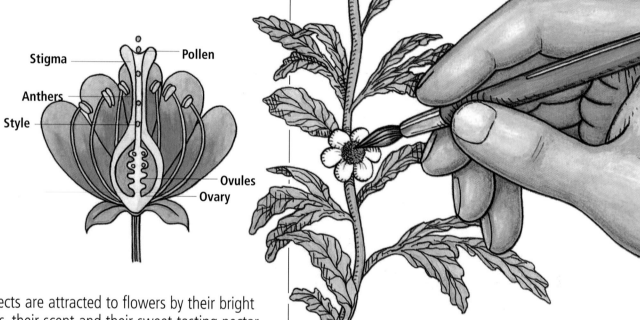

2 **When the flowers open**, you can use an artist's paint brush to transfer pollen from one flower to another. Push the brush into the flower and gently wiggle it about. Then push the brush into another flower and do the same thing.

3 **To test whether the pollen from another flower will fertilize the ovules**, first collect pollen from a different kind of flower – a geranium or a poppy for example – and pollinate one flower on the tomato plant. Tie a bit of cotton loosely round its stalk so that you can remember which flower you used for this test.

4 **Now pollinate the other tomato flowers** with tomato pollen. Use a clean paint brush every time you use a different sort of pollen.

5 **Carefully place a large, clear plastic bag over the plant** when you have finished pollinating, and tie it around the pot. This stops other pollens reaching the flowers.

6 **As soon as the flowers wither**, you can take the plastic bag off again.

7 **Which flowers develop into tomatoes?** The flowers with the cotton around the stalk that you pollinated with geranium pollen should not. If they do, it is because they were already pollinated with tomato pollen beforehand.

Scattering seeds

Flowers use many different methods to spread their seeds as widely as possible. Dandelions produce many seeds, each with its own parachute that is blown in the wind. Only a few will land where they can grow, but that is enough to ensure survival.

Some seeds have tiny hooks that cling to your clothes or to the fur of animals.

Many seeds are wrapped in tasty berries that are snapped up by birds and other animals. The berries are eaten but the seeds are dropped or they may pass right through the animal's body and start to grow miles away from the parent flower.

Lupins, vetches and other members of the pea and bean family have pods of seeds that burst open when they are ripe and scatter their seeds in all directions.

Poppy seeds are shaken from the capsule when it sways in the wind.

Seeds with burrs stick to clothes or fur.

Dandelion seeds have their own parachutes.

Berries are eaten by birds and animals and carried away by them.

Water-lily seeds float away from their parent plant.

Pea pods burst open to scatter their seeds.

Roadsides & Hedges

A roadside (or verge) is one of the best places for spotting wild flowers. As other habitats disappear, the roadside is one of the few places left for many plants to live in. The flowers you see here can tell you something about what the surrounding countryside was like originally.

In grassland areas, grassland flowers such as Scabious, Wild Parsnips and Lady's Bedstraws may grow along the roadside even after the meadows themselves have been ploughed and replanted. You may find Poppies and Ox-eye Daisies growing beside fields from which they have been removed by spraying. If a verge has lots of Bluebells, Celandines and Primroses, there was probably once a wood there.

Not all roadsides are thick with flowers. Some verges are cut like lawns and have only Yarrow and Dandelions. But if you find an undisturbed verge along a country lane, look for Queen Anne's Lace in early summer, and Cuckoo-pint and Toadflax later on. Motorway verges are also becoming wild-flower sanctuaries. Flowers can grow undisturbed in places like this because no one can stop and pick them.

Look out for hedges and hedge banks, not only beside roads, but also as boundaries between fields. Many hedges have been cut down to make fields bigger, but some have been in place for over a thousand years. The older the hedge is, the more different kinds of flowers you will see. Look for climbing plants, such as Honeysuckle and Bryony, and plants that like shade, such as Primroses and Hedge Woundwort. The picture shows six plants from this book; how many can you recognize?

White Campion, Meadow Crane's-bill, Herb Robert, Honeysuckle, Hogweed, Dog Rose

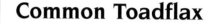

Greater Celandine

Although this plant belongs to the poppy family, it looks more like a buttercup. You can tell it isn't, however, because it has only four petals. The leaves are blue-green and divided into lobes. The stems are upright and very brittle. If you break one you will see the poisonous orange sap, which used to be used as a herbal remedy for warts. The flowers are followed by long, slender seed capsules.

Poppy family
Up to 1 m tall
Flowers from May to July

Common Toadflax

This plant is easy to recognize with its bright yellow-and-orange flower spike. It forms large colonies of upright stems with many narrow leaves. Look carefully at the flowers. Each has two lips with a straight spur and an orange 'tongue'. They are said to resemble a toad's mouth and so give the plant its name. In herbal medicine the plant is used to treat jaundice. Soaked in milk it makes a good fly poison.

Figwort family
30–90 cm tall
Flowers from July to September
Also grows in grassy places and on waste ground

Wild Parsnip

You will easily recognize this plant from its yellow umbrella-shaped flowerheads and its strong smell of parsnips. Look closely at one of the flowers. Each has five petals which roll inwards. The bright green leaves are pinnately divided into toothed leaflets. The stem is ridged and hollow. This plant is the wild form of the cultivated plant. The roots, which we eat, are the plant's food store.

Carrot family
Up to 1.5 m tall
Flowers from July to August
Also found in grassy waste places
Can blister skin if handled

Agrimony

The spikes of small yellow flowers grow at the tops of the stems. Look for the fruits which follow them. They have several rows of hooked bristles on the top which get tangled in the fur of passing animals – or in your clothes. The dark green leaves are deeply toothed and divided pinnately into many leaflets. Notice how large leaflets are mixed with small ones.

Rose family
30–60 cm tall
Flowers from June to September
Also grows in open woods and on the edges of fields

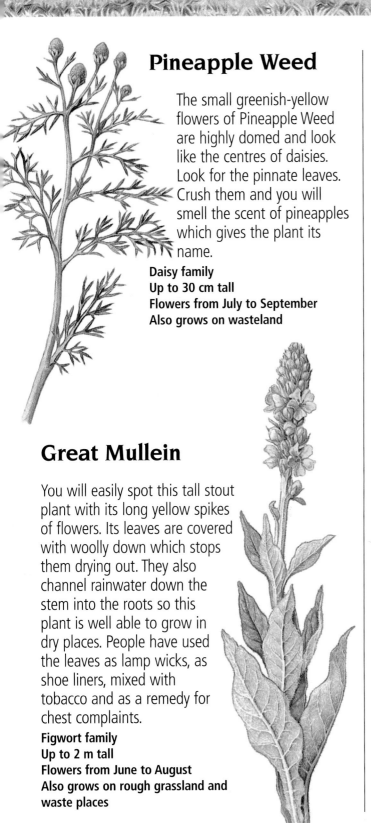

Pineapple Weed

The small greenish-yellow flowers of Pineapple Weed are highly domed and look like the centres of daisies. Look for the pinnate leaves. Crush them and you will smell the scent of pineapples which gives the plant its name.

Daisy family
Up to 30 cm tall
Flowers from July to September
Also grows on wasteland

Great Mullein

You will easily spot this tall stout plant with its long yellow spikes of flowers. Its leaves are covered with woolly down which stops them drying out. They also channel rainwater down the stem into the roots so this plant is well able to grow in dry places. People have used the leaves as lamp wicks, as shoe liners, mixed with tobacco and as a remedy for chest complaints.

Figwort family
Up to 2 m tall
Flowers from June to August
Also grows on rough grassland and waste places

Common Ragwort

You can tell Ragwort by its flat-topped clusters of golden yellow flowerheads. Look for the black-tipped bracts that cup the flowerheads. The leaves are dark green and deeply divided. They sometimes have cottony hairs underneath. They are followed by hairy seedheads which look rather like small dandelion clocks. All ragworts are poisonous to livestock and are dangerous when included in hay.

Daisy family
Up to 1.5 m tall
Flowers from June to October
Also grows in waste places, sand dunes and open woods

Creeping Buttercup

You will have no difficulty recognizing this well-known plant with its glossy yellow flowers, as a buttercup. What is more difficult, is to tell it from other buttercups, such as Meadow Buttercup (see page 54). Look at the way it grows. Creeping Buttercup has creeping stems and rosettes of three lobed leaves.

Buttercup family
Up to 60 cm tall
Flowers from May to August
Also grows in damp meadows, woods and marshes and as a garden weed

Hedge Bindweed

This plant is very similar to Field Bindweed (see page 18) but the flowers are twice as big and the leaves are two to three times bigger. The flowers of Hedge Bindweed are sometimes pink but usually white. Look for the arrow-shaped leaves and the bell-shaped flowers, which give it its other name of Bellbine. Notice how the plant twines itself anti-clockwise around other plants.

Bindweed family
Stems up to 3 m long
Flowers from June to August
Also grows in woodlands and waste places

Creeping Cinquefoil

This plant has bright yellow flowers growing on the ends of long flowering stalks. Do not confuse it with buttercups. Look for its notched petals, brighter stamens and very different leaves, which give it its name. They are palmate with five fingers (cinque is 'French' for 'five'). Notice how the plant puts down new roots as the stem creeps along.

Rose family
Grows along the ground
Flowers from June to August

Traveller's Joy

Look for Traveller's Joy twining its long stems through hedges. It clings with its coiled leaf stalks, which have three or five, pointed, oval leaflets. The scented flowers have four greenish-white sepals which look like petals, and many white stamens. The fruits have long, grey, hairy plumes that give it its other name – Old Man's Beard.

Buttercup family
Up to 30 m tall
Flowers from June to August
Also grows in thickets and woodland edges

Silverweed

The flowers of Silverweed look like those of Creeping Cinquefoil. You can tell them apart by their leaves. Silverweed has pinnate leaves with pairs of toothed leaflets. Look for the small leaflets between the larger ones. The leaves are dark green above with silver hairs beneath. The plant has been used to treat mouth ulcers and other sores, and as a cosmetic to remove freckles and spots.

Rose family
Grows along the ground
Flowers from June to August
Likes damp places

Honeysuckle

Honeysuckle is well known for its beautiful smell, strongest in the evening when it attracts moths. The moths must have long tongues, however, to reach down the long tubes to the nectar. Look at the mouth of the creamy-yellow flowers. Four petal lobes form the top and one petal the bottom. The dark green leaves are oval and pointed. The flowers are followed by clusters of red berries.

Honeysuckle family
Climbing stems
up to 6 m long
Flowers from
June to
September
Also grown
in gardens

White Campion

Look for the clumps of stems with their white starry flowers. Look carefully at the flowers. The petals are notched or cleft and the sepals are sticky and hairy. White Campion is very similar to Red Campion (see page 47) and the two plants often fertilize each other, so you may see flowers of any shade of pink where they grow together. The oval leaves are soft and hairy.

Pink family
Up to 90 cm tall
Flowers from May to August
Also grows on cultivated land and
waste ground

White Bryony

This climbing plant has palmate leaves with long coiled tendrils which grow from the base of the leaves and cling to other plants. Clusters of flowers grow from the base of the leaves too. They each have five greenish-white petals with darker veins. If you look closely you will see that male and female flowers are on separate plants. Female flowers have a swollen seed box under the petals. They ripen into red berries. This is a poisonous herb.

Gourd family
Stems up to 4 m long
Flowers from June to September
Also grows in woods

Black Bryony

Although this climbing plant has a similar name to White Bryony, it is very different. It is highly poisonous, particularly the berries, so be very careful. The dark green, shiny leaves are pointed and heart shaped and have no tendrils. Instead, the stem itself twines around other plants. The yellowish-green flowers grow in spikes, male and female flowers on separate plants. Female flowers are followed by bright red berries.

Yam family
Stems 2–4 m long
Flowers from May to July
Also grows in woods

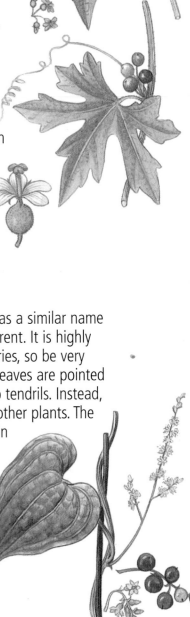

Roadsides & Hedges

Hedge Bedstraw

You will often see this plant tangled among the grasses at the base of a hedge bank. It has weak stems with many branches. The small, white flowers form loose, branched clusters. The leaves are oblong to oval and grow in whorls up the stems. The dry, black fruits grow in pairs.

Bedstraw family
Up to 30–150 cm tall
Flowers from June
to September
Also grows in woods
and waste places

Yarrow

Look for the more or less flat clusters of small white or pink flowerheads. Look too for the soft, ferny, dark green leaves. Yarrow grows tall in shady places, but keeps close to the ground on exposed ground. Yarrow has been used to dress wounds since the time of the ancient Greeks. It has an aromatic smell and today yarrow tea is a herbal remedy for colds.

Daisy family
Up to 45 cm tall
Flowers from July to August
Grows in grassy places

Cow Parsley

This is one of the commonest plants along the roadside. You will easily spot its white umbrella-shaped flower heads. It is also called Queen Anne's Lace after the frothy flowers which look like lace. Look carefully at those on the outer edge. One petal is larger than the rest. The leaves and leaflets are pinnate. After the flowers come the black and bristly fruits.

Carrot family
Up to 1 m tall
Flowers from May to June
Also grows in woodlands and waste places

Horse Radish

Horse Radish is best known for its roots which are used to make horseradish sauce. It sends up new, leafy shoots from its long tap roots with large, oblong, toothed leaves and does not always produce flowers. When it does flower, it sends up a tall, erect stem with many white flowers in a spreading, branched flowerhead. They are followed by round, globe-shaped fruits.

Mustard family
Up to 120 cm tall
Flowers from May to June
Also grows in fields and waste places

Garlic Mustard

You can best recognize this plant from the smell of garlic, which is strongest when you crush its leaves. The leaves are toothed and heart shaped with long stalks. They can be used in sauces instead of garlic, or chopped into salads. The white flowers grow in a dense cluster at the top of the stem. They give way to long, curved pods.

Mustard family
Up to 1 m tall
Flowers from April to June
Also grows in open woods

Field Pepperwort

These plants have tiny, white flowers growing in long spikes at the end of the stems. Look for fruits on the lower part while the top is still in bloom. The fruits are round and notched and become covered with white scales as they age. The lower leaves are lance shaped but become triangular higher up the stem. The young shoots can be chopped up and added to salads like watercress.

Mustard family
Up to 60 cm tall
Flowers from May to August
Grows in dry, grassy places

White Deadnettle

This plant looks very like Stinging Nettle (see page 10) but this one is called Deadnettle because it does not sting. You can tell them apart by their flowers. Stinging Nettle has clusters of green flowers which hang down under the leaves. White Deadnettle has large white flowers which grow above each pair of leaves. Apart from the colour of their flowers, White Deadnettle is very similar to Red Deadnettle (see page 18).

Mint family
Up to 60 cm tall
Flowers from April to September
Also grows in waste places

Hogweed

It is difficult to miss this tall, stout plant. The large umbrella-shaped flowerheads measure up to 20 cm across. The flowers may be white, greenish-white or pinkish. The outer ones have larger notched petals, which point outwards. The leaves are large too, and pinnate with lobed, toothed leaflets. The young leaves and shoots can be eaten as a vegetable.

Carrot family
Up to 2 m tall
Flowers from June to September
Also grows in rough grassy places and woodlands

Common Mallow

This plant has pink-purple flowers growing in clusters on hairy, sprawling clumps. The petals are veined with purple. The toothed leaves have 3–7 lobes and long stalks. Look for the wrinkled, brown-green fruits which follow the flowers. They look like round cheeses cut into segments.

Mallow family
Up to 90 cm tall
Flowers from June
to September
Also grows in waste
places and grassland

Blackberry

Blackberries are well known for their sweet, juicy berries. If you have picked them you will have noticed that the leaf stalks and stems of blackberry are prickly. The stems often grow about 1–2 m long, then arch over and root at the tips. The leaves have 3–5 toothed, oval leaflets. The flowers are white or pink and are followed by the fruit. Each section of the blackberry contains a seed.

Rose family
Stems up to 2 m long
Flowers from June
to September
Also found on heathland
and in woods

Upright Hedge-parsley

This is one of the three most common plants with white umbrella-shaped flowers that you are likely to see by the roadside – the other two are Cow Parsley and Hogweed (see pages 30 and 31). The best way to tell Upright Hedge Parsley from Cow Parsley is by the flowering time – Cow Parsley flowers earlier in the year. The flowers are followed by egg-shaped fruits covered with hooked spines.

Carrot family
Up to 1.2 m tall
Flowers from July to August

Hedge Woundwort

The flowers are dullish red with white markings. They grow in whorls and form a spike at the end of the stem. The leaves are heart shaped with toothed edges. They have an unpleasant smell when crushed and can be used as an antiseptic. They were once made into poultices to bind round wounds.

Mint family
Up to 1 m tall
Flowers from
July to August
Also grows in woods and shady places

Red Valerian

Look for the showy red flowerheads of this plant, growing on old walls or on cliffs and rocks. It was originally brought to this country from the Mediterranean as a garden flower. The leaves are grey-green and look rather waxy. They are oval to lance shaped. Those higher up the stem are sometimes toothed.

Valerian family
Up to 80 cm tall
Flowers from June to August
Also grown in gardens

Herb Robert

Look for this plant with its small, pink flowers growing on old walls or among other plants on the roadside. You can tell Herb Robert apart from other similar plants by its leaves. They are triangular and deeply lobed and look almost ferny. They turn red in the sun and later in the summer, and have a distinctive, unpleasant smell when rubbed.

Geranium family
Up to 30 cm tall
Flowers from May
to October
Also grows in woods
and on shingle coasts

Mugwort

It is easy to overlook this rather dull-looking plant. You are most likely to notice its deeply cleft leaves, which are smooth and dark green above, but white with cottony hairs below. The small flowerheads are reddish-brown and grow on long stems from the base of the leaves. The plant has a strong smell and is used as a herbal remedy for digestive problems.

Daisy family
Up to 120 cm tall
Flowers from July to September
Also grows in waste places

Dog Rose

You can tell this is a rose by its heart-shaped petals, thorny stems and pinnate leaves with toothed, oval leaflets. Like all wild roses, the flowers have five petals and sepals and many stamens in the centre. Look for the fruits – the bright red oval-shaped hips are rich in Vitamin C. They can be made into syrup or wine.

Rose family
Up to 3 m tall
Flowers from June to July
Also grows in woods

Germander Speedwell

This plant has some of the bluest flowers in the world. They grow in loose spikes at the end of long stalks. The oval leaves are toothed and grow in pairs up the stem. As well as upright stems, all speedwells have creeping stems that put down new roots to form a spreading mat of plants.

Figwort family
20–40 cm tall
Flowers from April to July
Also grows in woods, grassy places and as a garden plant

Meadow Crane's-bill

You cannot miss the large, blue, bowl-shaped flowers of this plant. They are over 35 mm across and grow in pairs at the end of long flower stems. The leaves are palmate. Look out for the fruits. Each one has 5 spoon-shaped sections. The seeds are in the bowls and all the handles form a 'beak'. When the seeds are ripe, the handles contract and the bowls fling out the seeds.

Geranium family
30–90 cm tall
Flowers from June to August
Also grows in meadows and as a garden plant

Woody Nightshade

You are most likely to see this climbing plant scrambling over shrubs or fences. Its blue-purple flowers have yellow centres and grow in loose clusters. They are followed by berries, which are green at first, then ripen to red. These berries are poisonous. The plant has long been used as a herbal remedy to treat skin diseases, asthma and whooping cough.

Nightshade family
Up to 2 m tall
Flowers from June to September
Also grows in waste places, often near the coast

Teasel

Teasels have upright prickly stems and prickly leaves. The lower leaves join across the stem making a cup to collect water and drown insects who might attack the plant. The tiny, pale purple flowers grow together in a cone-shaped head. The lower flowers open first so a purple 'band' appears to travel up the head. The dead dried flowerheads are visible all winter.

Teasel family
Up to 2 m tall
Flowers from June to August
Also grows in wet places and in woods

Sheep's-bit

Although this plant belongs to the Bellflower family, its flowers are not at all bell-like. It looks more like a scabious (see page 59). Its tiny blue flowers are gathered together in a round, flat head at the end of a bare long stalk. Notice the purple anthers sticking out from the head. Leafy bracts cup each flowerhead. The leaves are short and narrow and grow at the bottom of the stem.

Bellflower family
Up to 50 cm tall
Flowers in summer
Also grows on sandy
banks and cliffs

Tufted Vetch

This is probably the most common vetch. Notice how the bluish-purple flowers grow in a spike on one side of the stem only. The leaves are pinnate with pairs of small leaflets. Look for the branched tendrils at the end of the leaves. Vetches are scrambling plants and the tendrils twine around anything they touch. The flowers are followed by squarish pods which crack open in the hot sun to release the seeds.

Pea family
Up to 1 m tall
Flowers from June to August

Ivy-leaved Toadflax

Look for this plant growing on old walls and sometimes on rocks. The little flowers are blue-mauve with yellow centres. They grow from the base of the leaves which are rather thick and palmate, like ivy. Notice how the purplish, trailing stems put down new roots from time to time.

Figwort family
Up to 60 cm tall
Flowers from June to September
Also grown in gardens

Field Scabious

The flat, lilac-blue flowerheads of this plant are hard to miss among short grass. Notice how the outer, larger flowers form a ring around the head. It has rosettes of lance-shaped leaves, divided pinnately into lobes. The plant is called scabious because it was once used as a remedy for skin diseases like scabies.

Teasel family
Up to 1 m tall
Flowers from July to September
Grows in rough, dry, grassy places,
especially in chalky ground

Growing Your Own

Instead of picking flowers from the wild, why not grow your own in pots, window boxes or in your garden. Look for packets of wild flower seeds in your local garden centre. When they flower you can pick as many as you like.

Creating a wilderness

Birds and insects love weeds and wild plants. Ask your parents if you can turn a special corner of your garden into a wilderness. All you have to do is leave it to run wild. Let the grass grow and soon you will have dandelions, buttercups, clover and other common flowers growing there too.

Whatever you do, don't weed it! Buy a packet of wild flower seeds and scatter them there as well. Leave any fallen leaves to rot. Put some old logs and big stones in there too.

Then sit back and watch. Woodlice and other bugs will soon move in on the old leaves and logs. Birds will come to feed on them. In the summer bumble-bees, butterflies and other insects will pollinate the flowers.

Keep a record of the flowers that grow and the animals that visit it. If you can, make a small pond and grow water plants in it. You may soon find tadpoles and frogs in there too.

Grow flowers from bulbs

Many of the earliest spring flowers grow from bulbs. The bulb is a store of food that lets the plant shoot up and grow before it is warm enough for most flowers. **Only use bulbs that you can buy – never dig up bulbs that are growing wild.**

1 **Buy your bulbs in the autumn** and plant them in pots of compost, or garden soil mixed with sand. Dampen the compost before you begin.
2 **Half-fill the pot with soil or compost**, then plant the bulbs with the pointed end upwards. Leave about 2 cm between them. Cover them with soil until only the tips show.
3 **Leave the bulbs in a dark airy place** until they begin to grow. Don't forget about them and make sure you keep the compost damp.
4 **You should see the first shoots** in about two months. Put the pots in a warm, sunny place and water them. Try planting seeds from apples or oranges, and the stones from avocados or peaches as well. Plant them as above, put them on a window sill and keep them well watered.

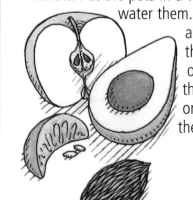

Hidden seeds

You can grow a surprise garden from the seeds you pick up on your boots on a muddy walk.

1 **Put on your boots and take a walk** after rainfall. It doesn't matter where you go, as long as it's muddy.

2 **Scrape the mud from your boots** when you get home, and put it in a clean jar or plastic container. Mix in enough water with the mud to make it runny and leave the mixture to soak overnight.

3 **Meanwhile half fill a metal tray or baking dish with garden soil** or compost and put it in the oven. Heat the oven to 200° Centigrade and bake the soil for 30 minutes. This will kill any seeds that are in it already. Leave it to cool overnight.

4 **Alternatively** you can buy sterile compost from a garden centre.

5 **Next day add the mud and water mixture** to the baked soil. Cover the tray with a sheet of clear plastic and store it in a warm place.

6 **The seedlings will begin to grow** after two or three weeks. As they get larger, carefully move them to bigger pots so you can watch them grow to full size.

7 **Can you identify all the plants?** Use this book to help you name them.

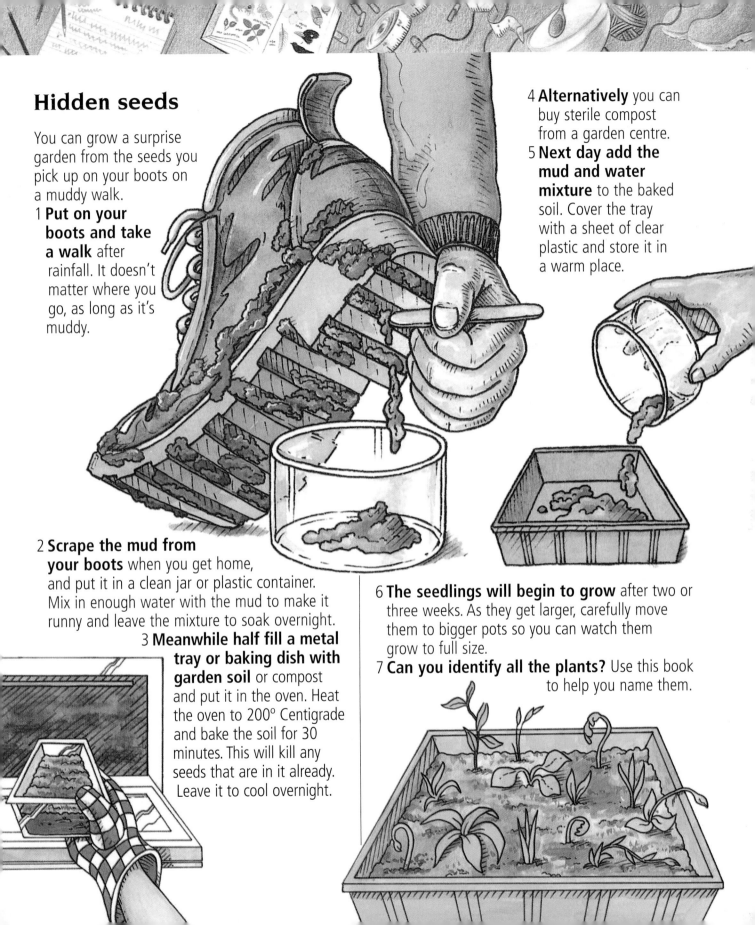

Woodlands

Oak, beech, ash and birch form most of the natural woodland of Britain. These are trees that lose their leaves in winter. When they are in full leaf in summer they create dense shade, but in late winter and spring, when the trees are bare or in bud, there is lots of light. Many woodland plants grow and flower at this time of the year. They die back in summer and lie under the ground until the next spring.

Most of these plants, such as Bluebells, Primroses, Wood Anemones and Ramsons, are perennials. They grow year after year from a bulb, rhizome or tuber, which stores enough food and energy to last the plant all winter. In summer look for woodland flowers in clearings or along paths where the sunlight reaches the ground between the trees. Here you may find Sanicle, Enchanter's Nightshade and Wood Avens.

Different kinds of woods grow in different parts of the country and different kinds of soil. In lowland England, Ireland and Wales the woods are mostly oak or beech. In wetter places, you may find alder and willow, and in sandy soils birch and pine. In Scotland the woods are mainly pine and birch.

Huge areas of coniferous trees have been planted across the British Isles. Their needle-like leaves stay on the trees all year, and their shade is so dense nothing grows beneath them. Very young or very old coniferous woods of spruce, larch and pine may not grow so thickly, so it is worth looking for wild flowers in them. The picture shows five plants from this book; how many can you identify?

Wood Anemone, Bluebell, Lesser Celandine, Primrose, Wood Sorrel

Woodlands

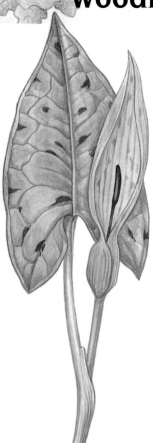

Cuckoo-pint

You are most likely to spot this plant in late summer, when you will see its thick stalk of bright red berries. Be careful: they are very poisonous. The large shiny green leaves first appear in spring. They are arrow shaped and often spotted with black. The leaves are followed by a large pale, yellow-green leafy bract which protects the dull-purple flower spike.

Arum family
30–60 cm tall
Flowers from April to May
Also found in woods

Cleavers

Cleavers has many common names, including Goosegrass, and is easy to recognize from its whorls of narrow, bristly leaves and round fruits. The fruits are covered in tiny hooks that catch on to anything that brushes against them. The young shoots can be eaten raw in salads or cooked as a vegetable. The fruits can be roasted as a substitute for coffee.

Bedstraw family
Up to 120 cm tall
Flowers from June to August
Grows in damp, shady places everywhere

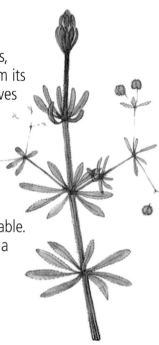

Twayblade

These small yellow-green flowers grow on short stalks in a slender spike at the end of the stem. Notice how the petals and sepals join together to make an open hood with a long, notched petal dangling below. Look for the single pair of rounded leaves near the base of the stem.

Orchid family
Up to 60 cm tall
Flowers from June to July

Broad-leaved Helleborine

The flowers of Helleborines grow on short stalks in long spikes on one side of the stem only. Look carefully at one of the flowers. The petals are purple with a heart-shaped lip, which varies in colour from purple to greenish-white. The leaves are broad and oval. They grow up the stem in a spiral. The largest leaves are about halfway up the stem.

Orchid family
Up to 80 cm tall
Flowers from July to September

Moschatel

This plant gets its name from its musky scent. It is also called Townhall Clock and Five-faced Bishop after its extraordinary flowerheads. Each has five yellow-green flowers, four of them forming a square and the fifth on top, facing the sky. The plant has clumps of light-green, three-lobed leaves. Each flower stem has a leaf about halfway up it.

Moschatel family
Up to 30 cm tall
Flowers in
early summer
Also grows in
hedgerows

Dog's Mercury

This poisonous plant grows in large, spreading colonies in woods. It has lance-shaped leaves with toothed edges. They grow in pairs up the upright stems. When they are crushed they smell of rotting fish. The flowers are green. Look for the male and female flowers, which grow on separate plants. The female flowers grow singly or in small clusters on large stalks. The male flowers form erect spikes.

Spurge family
15–40 cm tall
Flowers from February to April
Also grows in shady hedgerows

Common Figwort

Look for the many small flowers of this plant growing on lots of branches at the top of an upright stem. They have a greenish tube, but it is there brown upper lip which will probably catch your eye. Watch out for wasps, which are attracted to their unpleasant smell. The leaves grow in pairs; they are oval, pointed and sharply toothed.

Figwort family
Up to 80 cm tall
Flowers from June
to September
Grows in damp places
and beside streams

Wood Sage

This plant forms long spikes of yellow-green flowers which grow above a clump of branched stems with wrinkled leaves. Look carefully at the flowers. They have hanging lips and arching, brown stamens. The sage-green leaves are heart shaped and feel rough like sage leaves. They used to be dried and made into a tea which was used as a remedy for rheumatism and to clean sores.

Mint family
Up to 60 cm tall
Flowers from July
to September
Also grows on heaths,
dunes and shingle

Woodlands

Barren Strawberry

Barren Strawberry leaves are blue-green and divided into three toothed leaflets, just like those of Wild Strawberry. The flowers are also similar, but Barren Strawberry petals are heart-shaped while those of Wild Strawberry are rounded. Barren Strawberry also produces dry seed clusters instead of juice fruits. Both plants spread by producing runners. These creeping stems put down new roots and then new leaves and flowers grow from them.

Rose family
Up to 15 cm tall
Flowers from March to May
Also grows on roadsides
and grassy places

Primrose

Primroses are one of the best-known spring flowers. They have five heart-shaped, pale yellow petals. Look for the darker 'eye' at the centre. The flowers grow on hairy stalks from a clump of bright green, wrinkled, lance-shaped leaves. The leaves are paler underneath and covered with hairs.

Primrose family
Up to 25 cm tall
Flowers from
February to May
Also found in hedgerows
and on sunny banks

Yellow Archangel

Yellow Archangel looks very like White Deadnettle (see page 31) except the flowers are yellow rather than white. Look closely at one of the flowers. The upper petal is shaped like a helmet, while the lower petal is divided into three lobes and has red-brown streaks. After it has flowered, the plant often puts out creeping stems that root and produce new plants.

Mint family
Up to 60 cm tall
Flowers from May to June

Lesser Celandine

This plant has bright yellow flowers with 8–12 pointed petals which fade to white as they get older. Look for the three green sepals behind the petals. The leaves are heart shaped and glossy green. Both leaves and flowers grow on long stalks in a clump from an underground tuber.

Buttercup family
Up to 15 cm tall
Flowers from
March to May
Also grows beside
streams and on
damp roadsides

Wood Avens

Look for this plant with its small yellow flowers in damp, shady places. The leaves grow in clumps. Notice how each leaf has one large, middle leaflet with two smaller ones on each side. The flowers are followed by hooked burrs. If you look closely, you will see that the hooks are jointed and often point downwards.

Rose family
20–60 cam tall
Flowers from June to August
Also grows in hedgerows

Wild Strawberry

Wild Strawberries are smaller, but sweeter, than cultivated strawberries. The white flowers have five separate round petals. Look into the centre of the flower. The many stamens surround a green cone, which will eventually swell to form the strawberry. Look at a ripe strawberry and you can see the seeds embedded on the outside.

Rose family
Up to 30 cm tall
Flowers from
April to July
Also grows on scrub and in hedge banks

Perforate St John's-wort

The little yellow flowers of this plant grow in many large clusters at the top of the stem. Each flower has five pointed petals and many stamens. Look closely at the petals and you will see that they have tiny black dots around the edge. The leaves are linear and grow in pairs. If you hold one of the leaves up to the light you will see that it is covered by clear dots.

St John's-wort family
About 60 cm tall
Flowers from June to September
Also grows on roadsides and in meadows

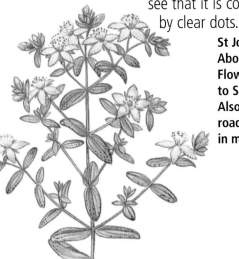

Wall Lettuce

Look for the tiny yellow flowers of this plant growing in large, spreading clusters at the top of an upright stem. Notice that each flowerhead has only five ray florets. The leaves are pinnately lobed and the end lobe is larger than the rest. The upper leaves are often reddish and clasp the stem at their base.

Daisy family
Up to 1 m tall
Flowers from July to August
Also grows on walls, hedge banks and waste places

Woodlands

Wood Sorrel

Look for Wood Sorrel growing on rotting trees or wherever there is plenty of humus. It forms carpets of bright green, clover-like leaves. They are each divided into three heart-shaped leaflets which fold down at night. The flowers grow singly, each on a long, bare stalk. They have five white petals streaked with violet.

Wood Sorrel family
Up to 15 cm tall
Flowers from April to May
Also grows in hedgerows and on shady banks

Snowdrop

The nodding, white flowers of this plant appear even before winter is over and the plants are among the first to bloom. Look closely at the flower. It has three spreading outer petals which are pure white, and three smaller, inner petals which are streaked with green and notched at the tips. The long, narrow leaves and flowering stems grow from small bulbs.

Lily family
Up to 25 cm tall
Flowers from January to March
Also grown in gardens

Greater Stitchwort

The bright, satiny-white flowers of this plant grow on weak, straggling stems which do not look strong enough to hold them. In fact, the brittle stems are often supported by other plants. Look closely at the flower. It has five petals, each split up to halfway down its length. The narrow, pointed leaves grow in pairs up the stem.

Pink family
Up to 60 cm tall
Flowers from April to June
Also grows in hedgerows

Ramsons

This plant has white, starry flowers growing in a flat-topped cluster at the end of the flowering stem. They grow from narrow bulbs with broad, bright green leaves. Two leaves and one flowering stem grow from each bulb. Where there are many plants together you will smell their slightly rancid, garlicky scent.

Lily family
About 30 cm tall
Flowers from May to June
Also grow in hedgerows and other shady places

Enchanter's Nightshade

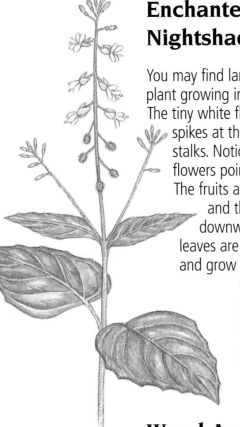

You may find large patches of this plant growing in shady places. The tiny white flowers form long spikes at the end of the stalks. Notice how the flowers point downwards. The fruits are bristly capsules and they point downwards too. The leaves are large and oval and grow in pairs.

Willowherb family
Up to 60 cm tall
Flowers from June to August
Also found in hedgerows

Wood Anemone

You will probably see Wood Anemones growing in large patches, perhaps with Bluebells (see page 46). Each white flower has 5–9 petal-like sepals. Look underneath the sepals. They are sometimes streaked with pink. Each stem has a whorl of three leaves about a third of the way down. Each leaf is divided palmately into five lobes.

Buttercup family
Up to 30 cm tall
Flowers from April to May

Sweet Woodruff

This is another woodland plant that grows from underground stems and forms carpets of leaves and flowers. The white flowers grow in branched clusters at the tops of the stems. Look for the whorls of 6–8 lance-shaped leaves. The plant smells of new-mown hay and keeps this sweet scent, even when dried. It was used in perfumes or was put in drawers and cupboards with clothes.

Bedstraw family
Up to 45 cm tall
Flowers in early summer

 ## Sanicle

The dense white or pink flowerheads of this plant grow in clusters at the ends of long stalks. Look for the clumps of shiny, palmate leaves. Look too for the fruits. They are covered with many hooked bristles, which can catch in your clothing or animals' fur. Sanicle was once an important medicinal herb, but now it is used only in gargles, and ointments for treating wounds.

Carrot family
Up to 60 cm tall
Flowers from May to August

Woodlands

Water Avens

Look for the bell-shaped flowers of this plant in wet places. They have orange-pink petals and purplish sepals. The flowers give way to many small, dry fruits with long hooks which catch in your clothing or animals' fur. The leaves have several pinnate leaflets, which get larger and broader towards the end of the leaf stalk.

Rose family
20–60 cm tall
Flowers from June to August
Also grows in marshes and beside streams

Early Purple Orchid

The flowers of this plant vary in colour from pale pink to bright purple. Look for the flowers in clusters at the end of the stalk. They grow from a rosette of lance-shaped leaves, which are usually covered with black spots. At first the flowers smell of vanilla, but after they have been pollinated the scent changes to become more like tomcats.

Orchid family
Up to 60 cm tall
Flowers from April to June

Bluebell

Bluebells look most spectacular in oak woods where they carpet the ground in April and May. The violet-blue flowers are bell shaped and grow in a spike on one side of the stem. Notice how the tips of the petals curve backwards. The plants grow from bulbs and they have many long, narrow grass-like leaves.

Lily family
Up to 50 cm tall
Flowers from April to May
Also grows in hedges

Foxglove

You cannot miss this plant, with its tall spike of hanging bells. The flowers are mauve-pink and the petals are joined together to make the bell-shaped tube. Look for the black spots inside the tube. The large, lance-shaped leaves are soft and hairy. They are poisonous and can cause heart failure if eaten. They contain the drug digitoxin, used in medicine to treat heart diseases.

Figwort family
1–2 m tall
Flowers from June to August
Also grows on mountains

Ground Ivy

Ground ivy is not an ivy at all, although it does creep along the ground, putting down roots from time to time. In spring and early summer the stems turn upwards. Look then for the blue-purple flowers which grow in twos or fours at the base of the leaves. The leaves are heart shaped and have wavy edges. The plant tastes bitter and was used in beer-making before hops were substituted. It is still used in herb medicine as a remedy for colds and diarrhoea.

Mint family
Stems up to 60 cm long
Flowers from
April to May
Also grows in hedge
banks and waste
places

Red Campion

This plant has rosy-red flowers, which are easy to spot. They have five notched petals and grow from a sticky tube formed by the joined-together sepals. The plant is closely related to White Campion (see page 29). The leaves are soft and hairy and grow in pairs up the stems which are sticky and hairy too.

Pink family
Up to 90 cm tall
Flowers from May to June
Also common in hedgerows

Common Dog Violet

Although this little violet is common, it is easy to miss among other plants. The petals are blue-violet with a paler, often whitish spur behind them. The flowers grow on their own stalks in the middle of a clump of leaves. The leaves are heart shaped and grow on long stalks too. This violet has no scent and is usually hairless.

Violet family
Only 15 cm tall
Flowers from
April to June
Also grows in
hedgerows

Experiments with Plants

Everyone knows plants need water and light. They take in water through their roots from the soil. But how does the water flow up from the roots to every other part of the plant? Also, watch plants turning to the light, and make water and oxygen.

Colouring a flower

This experiment shows how stems move water from the roots to the leaves and flowers.

1 **Take a white flower** – like a carnation, geranium, or Cow Parsley (see page 30) – and carefully split the lower part of its stem into two.
2 **Fill two small pots with water.** Colour one with red ink and the other with blue or another colour.
3 **Put one half of the stem** in one pot and the other half in the other pot. Leave it for an hour or two, or overnight.
4 **What happens to the flower?** Look at the split stem to see the tiny tubes (xylem) now coloured by the dyed water.

You can use any ink colour you like in these pots. Or you could mix two colours together (red and blue, for example, to make purple). But be careful – don't spill any on your clothes!

Plants lose water, too

Water is drawn up to the top of a plant by evaporation from tiny holes in the leaves. The holes, called stomata, open by day and allow water vapour to escape. More water then moves up to take its place. It is like water being sucked up through thousands of tiny drinking straws. The leaves use some of the water to make food, but most of it escapes through the stomata.

1 **Take a small potted plant** and water it well.
2 **Put a clear plastic bag over all the leaves.** Make sure your bag is large enough that it doesn't squash the leaves, then tie it firmly around the base of the stem.
3 **Leave it in a sunny spot.**
4 **After an hour or two** the inside of the bag will be covered with little drops of water that the plant has breathed out.

Striped celery

Do the same experiment with a stick of celery. When you cut across the stem, the red dots show the xylem (tiny tubes that carry water and nutrients up from the roots).

48

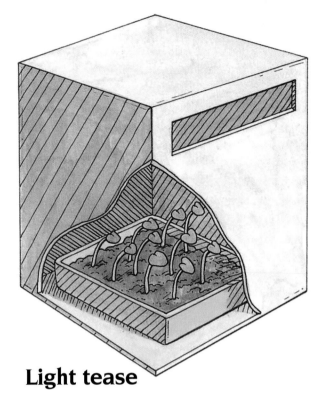

Light tease

Plants turn their leaves and grow towards the light. Put a potted plant near a window and in a day or so you will see that all its leaves are facing the light. Then turn it round. How long does it take for the leaves to turn to face the light again?

Most plants grow fairly straight up towards the light, but what happens if the light is coming only from one side?

1 **Take a large cardboard box** and cut a wide slit out of the bottom of one side (see the picture).
2 **Plant up a pot or tray of quick-growing seedlings**, such as bean sprouts or sunflowers.
3 **Put the box over the seedlings** so that no light gets in except from the slit.
4 **Put the whole experiment in a sunny place** with the slit facing the sun and leave it for a few days. What happens to the seedlings?
5 **You can tease them** by turning them round to face away from the slit. Put the box back in the sun and see what happens in the next few days.

Make an oxygen bubble

While leaves are making food, they also make oxygen. In fact much of the oxygen we breathe from the air has been made by plants. This experiment will show a plant making oxygen.

1 **Buy a few aquatic plants** from a pet shop that sells tropical fish.
2 **Fill a large glass, or clear plastic, container** or aquarium with water and put the plants in the bottom. Put it in a sunny place.
3 **Cut off the bottom of a large, clear plastic bottle**, take off its screw cap and place it over the plants.
4 **Balance a small glass over the top of the bottle** as shown in the picture. Make sure there is no air in the glass by holding it under water first.
5 **After a few days** you should notice a space at the top of the glass where the oxygen is collecting. You may even see bubbles rising from the plant.

Meadows & Pastures

Grasslands are open grassy areas with few trees or shrubs. They get plenty of sunlight and wind, but have little shelter. Nevertheless, many plants thrive here. Even slow-growing, rare plants can survive here undisturbed if the ground is used for grazing animals and never ploughed.

Lowland meadows and pastures have long grasses, while downs and limestone uplands have shorter grass. Lowland meadows are cut once a year in early summer for hay (preserved by drying) or silage (preserved by fermentation). Meadow flowers, such as Clovers, Buttercups and Ox-eye Daisies are well adapted to hay-making. They flower and set seed before the grass is cut.

Today many meadows and pastures have been ploughed up. Many others have been replanted with newer kinds of grass and the flowers have disappeared. The grass is often cut a few weeks earlier and stored as silage, before the flowers have had time to set seed.

Downs and limestone uplands have suffered a similar fate. For hundreds of years the South Downs, Salisbury Plain and limestone uplands in the Yorkshire Dales, the Peak District and the Mendips have been used for grazing sheep. Now most of the downs have been ploughed up and are used to grow cereals. If you are lucky enough to find an area with Rockroses, Thyme and Pyramidal Orchids, you are most likely on one of the few undisturbed areas left. The picture shows nine plants from this book; how many can you recognize?

Buttercup, Red and White Clover, Ragged Robin, Ribwort, Common Rockrose, Musk Thistle, Thyme, Bird's-foot Trefoil

Meadows & Pastures

Common Eyebright

Look for the spotted white flowers of this plant hidden among the leafy bracts at the tops of the stems. The upper lip of each flower is often streaked with purple and the lower lip has a yellow blotch. The oval, toothed leaves grow in pairs. Eyebright got its name because it was used in herbal medicine to treat sore and tired eyes.

Figwort family
Up to 50 cm tall
Flowers from June to September

Common Lady's Mantle

The flowers of Lady's Mantle grow in large clusters at the end of branched, leafy stalks. The leaves are palmate and hold drops of water after rain or heavy dew. Look closely at one of the flowers. It has no petals, only yellow-green sepals. Lady's Mantle is unusual because its seeds germinate without being pollinated.

Rose family
Up to 45 cm tall
Flowers from June to August
Also grows in woods and beside streams

White Clover

You can easily recognize White Clover from its leaves, which are divided into three rounded leaflets. Look for the white band around the base of each leaflet. The thick white or pale pink flowerheads grow from the base of the leaf stalk. All clovers are rich in nectar. Watch out for bees probing into the many small flowers that make up the flowerhead. Some of the best honey is made from clover.

Pea family
Up to 50 cm tall
Flowers from June to September
Often found on lawns

Ribwort

You cannot miss the tight green flowerheads of this plant growing among the grass. Look for the white stamens sticking out from the head. The leaves are lance-shaped and strongly ribbed with 3–7 heavy veins. The flower stems and leaves have long, silky hairs. Ribwort contains a mucilage, which is used in cough medicines.

Plantain family
Up to 45 cm tall
Flowers from April to July
Also grows on roadsides and waste ground

Wild Carrot

You will easily spot this plant, with its large flat umbels of creamy-white flowers. Look for the one purple or red flower in the centre of each umbel. The leaves are fern-like and grow in pairs. When the flowers die, the umbels close up and look like birds' nests with many spiky fruits. Wild Carrot does not have swollen fleshy roots like cultivated carrots, but it does smell like a carrot.

Carrot family
30–90 cm tall
Flowers in summer

Sheep's Sorrel

This plant has tiny flowers growing in whorls up the long, flowering stems. Their fruits are often easier to spot, especially when there are lots of them. They are tiny, three-sided, golden-brown nutlets. Look too at the leaves. They are shaped like spearheads with spreading lobes at the base. The leaves taste sour and can be eaten in salads or cooked as a vegetable. They can also be made into a drink.

Dock family
Up to 30 cm tall
Flowers from May to June

Hemlock

This plant is poisonous and was used to kill Socrates, the famous Greek philosopher. It has an unpleasant smell, rather like the strong smell of mice. The best way to tell it apart from other plants with umbels of small white flowers is to look at the stem. It is greyish and smooth with purple spots. The leaves are soft and divided into leaflets, which are themselves further divided into leaflets.

Carrot family
Up to 3 m tall
Flowers from June to July
Also grows on roadsides, in woods and beside streams

Goatsbeard

This plant has bright-yellow showy flowers and grass-like leaves. Look for the long bracts beneath the flowers, which are longer than the petals. It gets the name Goatsbeard from the seed heads. They form a large ball of feathery seeds, with long silky hairs. The flower is also called Jack-Go-To-Bed-At-Noon because its flowerheads close up at lunchtime.

Daisy family
About 60 cm tall
Flowers from June to July
Also grows on roadsides
and in waste places

Tormentil

Tormentil flowers look rather like small Buttercups (see below) or Creeping Cinquefoil (see page 28), but they have four heart-shaped petals, not five. Look for the leafy stems, trailing along the ground. The leaves are divided into five toothed leaflets, three large and two small. The two smaller ones are called 'stipules'.

Rose family
Stems only 10 cm long
Flowers from June to September

Meadow Buttercup

You will easily recognize the flowers of this well-known plant with its five glossy yellow petals as a Buttercup. It is easy to tell it apart from Creeping Buttercup (see page 27) because it does not have creeping stems. The leaves are palmate, but the middle lobe has no stalk. All buttercups are slightly poisonous and are avoided by cattle and other grazing animals who are put off by their burning, acrid taste.

Buttercup family
Up to 1 m tall
Flowers from May to July
Also grows near damp
roadsides and ditches

Cat's-ear

You may at first mistake these plants for dandelions, but their stems are quite different. Dandelions have smooth, hollow stems, while the stem of Cat's-ear is tough and solid with several flowers. Look closely to spot the small, dark bracts (tiny leaves) growing up it. The flowerheads, too, are cupped in overlapping bracts which look like scales.

Daisy family
Up to 60 cm tall
Flowers from June
to September
Also grows on roadsides

Lady's Bedstraw

This plant has wiry, creeping stems and forms large patches of leafy stalks with clusters of small yellow flowers. The leaves are narrow and grow in whorls.

Lady's Bedstraw is so called because it was said to be in the straw in the stable where Christ was born. It has been used for many things, including cheese-making, dyeing and herb medicine.

Bedstraw family
Up to 90 cm tall
Flowers from July to August
Also grows on roadsides
and hedge banks

Common Rockrose

This sprawling plant with its bright yellow flowers is easy to spot on dry grassland or grassy banks. Each flower has five overlapping petals and many yellow stamens. The petals soon fall and give way to capsules of seeds. The leaves grow in pairs. They are green above but covered with thick white hairs beneath.

Rockrose family
Up to 30 cm tall
Flowers from July to August
Also grown in rock gardens

Bird's-foot Trefoil

The bright yellow flowerheads of this plant are often tinged with red and grow on long stalks from the base of the leaves. Each small leaf has three leaflets. Look out for the long seed pods. When they are dry and ripe, they twist and split open to release the seeds. The plant has many other names, including Eggs-and-Bacon, Cat's Claw and Devil's Fingers.

Pea family
Up to 30 cm tall
Flowers from June
to August

Cowslip

You can easily recognize this plant because the leaves are similar to Primroses (see page 42). Cowslip flowers, however, grow in a drooping cluster at one side of the single flowering stalk. Look too for the orange spots in the centre of each flower. Cowslips have a sweet scent, but do not pick them because they are becoming quite rare.

Primrose family
Up to 30 cm tall
Flowers from April
to May
Also grows on grassy
banks and roadsides

Meadows & Pastures

Wild Marjoram

This plant grows in patches, with dense clusters of reddish-purple or pale pink flowers. Look for the butterflies and bees, which are attracted to them. The flowerheads grow from the base of the leaves. The leaves are oval shaped and grow in pairs up the upright stems. Crush one and smell the strong scent of Marjoram, which is used as a herb in cooking. The plant is also called Oregano.

Mint family
About 60 cm tall
Flowers from July to September
Also found in hedge banks, roadsides and scrub

Wild Thyme

Look for this plant growing close to the ground. Many flowering stems grow from the main shoot and end with a purple flowerhead. Look closely to see that each tiny flower has two lips. The leaves are small and oval shaped, and grow in pairs along the stems. Their scent is like the herb, Garden Thyme, but weaker.

Mint family
Grows along the ground
Flowers from June to August
Grows in dry, grassy places

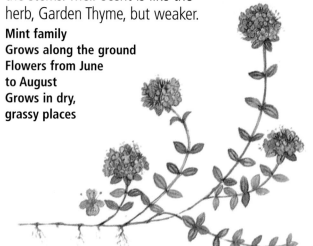

Cuckoo-flower

Look for the flowers of this plant in late spring when the cuckoo starts to call. Another name for it is Lady's Smock. It produces a cluster of delicate lilac-pink flowers. Look at the leaves. Those of the stem are divided pinnately into narrow leaflets, but the rosette of leaves round the base has oval-shaped leaflets. The seed pods which follow the flowers are long and flat.

Mustard family
About 60 cm tall
Flowers from April to June
Grows in damp, grassy places

Pyramidal Orchid

This is one of the commonest orchids found in Europe. You can recognize it from the pyramid-shape of its flowerhead when young. As all the flowers begin to open, it becomes more cylindrical. The flowers are deep rose-purple and scented. The leaves are narrow and lance shaped. Those at the bottom of the stem are largest, and hide the bottom of the stem.

Orchid family
About 45 cm tall
Flowers from June to August
Also found in open scrub and woodland

Red Clover

Red Clover has dark red-pink flowers, while White Clover has pale pink or white flowers (see page 52). Also, Red Clover has narrow pointed leaflets. The pink-purple flowerheads grow between two leaves at the ends of the stems. Clover petals stay on the flowerhead after they have withered. Look then for the seed pods in the brown flowerheads.

Common Spotted Orchid

You can recognize this plant from the black spots on the leaves. It has a spike of flowers at the end of the stem. The flowers vary in colour from white to bright reddish-purple. Look for their symmetrical pattern of lines and blotches. The leaves are narrow and lance shaped. Notice how they get narrower and shorter as they go up the stem.

Orchid family
Up to 15–50 cm tall
Flowers from June to September
Also found in open woods and scrub

Ragged Robin

It is easy to recognize this plant from its 'ragged', rose-red flowers. Look closely to see how the petals are split into narrow strips, giving them their ragged look. The leaves are lance shaped and grow in pairs up the stems. Notice how the plant has both sprawling leafy stems and upright flowering stems.

Pink family
Up to about 75 cm tall
Flowers from May to June
Grows in damp, grassy places

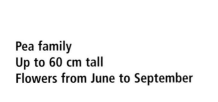

Pea family
Up to 60 cm tall
Flowers from June to September

Lesser Knapweed

The flowers of Knapweeds look like those of thistles, but the leaves and stems have no spines or prickles. The stems are tough and upright and the leaves are long and lobed. The red-purple flowerheads grow at the ends of the stems. The seedbox is covered with overlapping, triangular bracts and gives the plant its other name – Hardheads.

Daisy family
Up to 60 cm tall
Flowers from July to September
Grows on dry grassland and on cliffs and roadsides

Felwort

This plant is also called Autumn Gentian. Its clusters of flowers may be reddish-purple, dull purple, blue, pink or white. The petals form a tube then spread out into four or five separate tips. Look for the fringe of hairs inside the flower. The leaves are oval to lance shaped and grow in pairs up the stem.

Gentian family
About 30 cm tall
Flowers from August to September
Also found on sand-dunes and cliffs

Stemless Thistle

As its name implies, this thistle has no stalk. Its flat rosettes of spiny, lobed leaves are often hidden among the grasses. Sometimes it is so widespread on the grassy downs that it is difficult to find a comfortable place to sit. A single bright red-purple flower grows in the centre of each rosette.

Daisy family
Ground-level
Flowers from July to September

Harebell

The light blue, nodding, bell-shaped flowers of this plant are easy to spot on their slender stems. Notice how the five petals are joined to make the 'bell'. The leaves are long and narrow. This delicate flower is known as Bluebell in Scotland, but is also called Old Man's Bells and Lady's Thimbles.

Bellflower family
No more than 40 cm tall
Flowers from July to August
Also grows on dry grassland and dunes

Musk Thistle

You will easily tell this plant is a thistle from its spiny leaves and stalk. Look for Musk Thistle's drooping purple flowerhead. It grows on its own or in small clusters at the top of the stems. Notice that the spiny wings on the stems stop some distance below the flowerhead. The seeds have long, whitish hairs.

Daisy family
Up to 1 m tall
Flowers from June to September
Also found in waste places and on roadsides

Green-winged Orchid

It is easy to tell that this plant is an orchid, with its distinctive flowers and lance-shaped leaves that clasp the stem. Look closely at one of the flowers. It has a spreading helmet marked with green veins and this gives the flower its name. The helmet is folded over the reddish-purple, three-lobed lip.

Orchid family
Up to 40 cm tall
Flowers from May to June
Also grows on banks and roadsides

Devil's-bit Scabious

Look for this plant growing in wet meadows, marshes and fens. You will easily notice its mauve or blue-purple flowerhead. Notice how all the flowers in the head are the same size, even those around the edge. The stem grows from a rosette of long, oval-shaped leaves. Only a few, narrow leaves grow up the stem too.

Teasel family
Up to 1 m tall
Flowers from June to September

Common Restharrow

Look for these pinkish-purple flowers growing from leafy, woody stems close to the ground. The flowers grow in loose spikes, with each flower growing from the base of a leaf. The leaves are divided into three leaflets, like clover. Look closely to see how the veins end in teeth round the edge of the leaflet.

Pea family
About 60 cm tall
Flowers from June to August
Grows in rough, grassy places

Preserving Wild Flowers

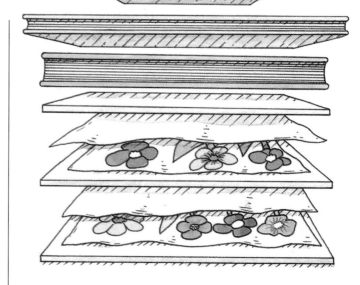

Most wild flowers soon wither if you pick them, but you can preserve them for a long time by pressing or drying them. Only pick flowers that you know are common. Start with wild flowers from your garden, and don't pick more than one. Remember to choose a stem with a leaf or take a separate leaf to press.

Flat flowerheads like Evening Primrose, Violet, Wild Strawberry, Buttercup and Forget-me-not press well. Avoid very bulky flowerheads like Clover or Teasel. It is much better to dry them. Take a plastic bag with you to put the flowers in. It will help to keep them fresh until you get home.

Pressing flowers

You can buy a flower press ready-made or you can make your own. You will need paper towels, cardboard or newspaper, and several heavy books. You can use out-of-date phone books or any heavy books like encyclopedias. Choose a warm, dry room to make your press and a table or cupboard where it can remain undisturbed for two or three weeks.

1 **Arrange the flowers and leaves carefully** on the sheets of paper towel. Give each flower enough room and remember it will press dry just as you have put it.

2 **Start with a piece of cardboard** or four layers of folded newspaper on a flat hard surface. Lay a paper towel with flowers on top of it. Put another sheet of paper towel and then cardboard or folded newspaper on top of it.

3 **Go on adding layers of flowers** between paper towels and cardboard or newspaper until you have a stack no more than 15 cm high. Finish with a cardboard or newspaper layer.

4 **Carefully place the heavy books on top of the stack.**

5 **Leave the flowers alone for two weeks.** Then peel the paper back gently and check that the flowers are flat and dried. If they are not, leave them for another week.

Drying flowers

Drying is even better then pressing for preserving wild flowers. It keeps their shape as well as their colour, and in some cases dried flowers are hard to tell from fresh ones.

Members of the daisy family, such as daisies, thistles and dandelions all dry well. Field Scabious and roses are good too. Always pick the flowers just before they are in full bloom.

Don't pick any flowers that are beginning to fade or wither, unless of course you wait until they go to seed. Poppies, teasels and many other seed heads look very attractive dried. So do grasses.

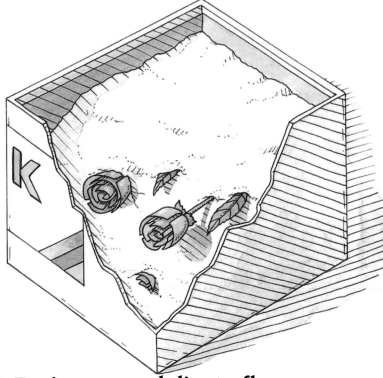

Air drying

The easiest way to dry flowers is by tying them into a bunch with a rubber band then hanging them upside-down in a dry, airy place for a few weeks. An airing cupboard is ideal because you can hang them up easily. An attic, spare room or garage is also fine but you will need to fix up a pole or line to hang them from. Don't put too many flowers into each bunch.

Drying more delicate flowers

Some flowers lose some of their shape and colour if they are simply air-dried. It is better to dry roses, lilies, and anemones using a mixture of oat or wheat bran (buy it from a supermarket or health shop) and laundry borax (buy it from a chemist).

1 **Find a box**, such as a shoe box, which is large enough to hold the flowers easily.
2 **Mix equal parts of borax and bran** together, enough to fill half the box.
3 **Pour some of the mixture into the box** to make a layer 2.5 cm deep.
4 **Cut the flower stems** so that they fit into the box and carefully arrange the flowers on top of the mixture without overlapping each other.
5 **Gently sprinkle more of the mixture over the flowers** until they are covered by a layer about 2.5 cm deep.
6 **After a week**, take the flowers out of the box very carefully as they are fragile, and dust off the drying mixture with an artist's paintbrush.

Rivers, Ponds & Lakes

Wetlands include a variety of habitats, from small ponds and ditches to streams, rivers, lakes, marshes, fens and wet woods. Some plants grow only in the still water of ditches or ponds, while others prefer flowing water in streams or rivers.

All wetland plants need constant water, but vary in how much of the plant needs to be submerged. Notice which ones have only their roots in water, which grow almost completely underwater with only their leaves floating on the surface, and which are wholly submerged.

True water plants have a different internal structure from other plants. They may rely on the water, rather than their stems, to support them. Some of their leaves and stems may contain large air spaces to help them float. The picture shows six plants from the book; how many can you recognize?

Arrowhead, Bulrush, Meadowsweet, Monkeyflower, White Water-lily, Great Hairy Willowherb

Tubular Water-dropwort

Look for this plant with its dense umbels of white flowers growing at the ends of hollow stems. Notice how the stems are pinched in where they branch or the leaf stalks grow. The leaves are pinnate with pairs of narrow leaflets. You will not see the roots, but they are swollen, more so at one end than the other. The umbels of flowers give way to globules of fruit. Be careful – this plant is poisonous.

Carrot family
30–90 cm tall
Flowers from July to September
Grows in marshes and shallow water

Watercress

Look for this plant in the quiet waters of streams and springs. It has dark green leaves, divided pinnately into rounded leaflets. The spikes of white flowers grow at the ends of hollow stalks. They are followed by upright cylindrical pods of seeds. Look closely to see the outlines of the seeds inside them. The leaves of Watercress are rich in Vitamins A and C. They are good to eat in salads.

Mustard family
Up to 60 cm tall
Flowers from May to September

Meadowsweet

The creamy-white flowerheads of this plant contain many tiny sweet-scented flowers. Their long stamens make them look fluffy. The dark green leaves grow in clumps. They are divided pinnately into toothed leaflets. Look for the pairs of smaller leaflets between the larger ones. Look for the fruits. The seed case twists itself into a spiral.

Rose family
60–120 cm tall
Flowers from July to August
Grows in wet meadows, marshes, wet woods and on river banks

Fool's Watercress

This plant often grows with Watercress and the leaves of the two plants are alike. It is not poisonous, however, in spite of its name, and it can be eaten. The leaves are bright green and shiny. They are divided pinnately into oval leaflets. The umbels of white flowers (quite different from those of Watercress) grow on several short stalks at the end of the ridged stem.

Carrot family
30–90 cm tall
Flowers from June to August
Grows in shallow ponds and ditches

Common Water-crowfoot

Look for the small white flowers of this submerged plant sticking up above the water. The plant has two kinds of leaves – one that floats on the water, and another that grows below the surface. The floating leaves have three or five toothed lobes. Those beneath the water are finely dissected and grow on long submerged stems. The flowers give way to rounded seed heads which bend back into the water.

Buttercup family
Flowers from June to August
Grows in ponds, ditches and small streams

White Water-lily

The beautiful white flowers of this Water-lily float on the water. They open in the morning and close in the late afternoon. The round leaves float too. They grow on long stalks from the underground stem in the mud below. As the flowers wither, their long stalks coil and pull them under the water so the seed capsules ripen there. When the capsules burst, the seeds rise to the surface and float away.

Water-lily family
Flowers from June to August
Grows in still or slow-moving water

Common Water-plantain

Look for the tall flowering stems reaching high out of the water. They have whorls of small, white or pink flowers. Notice that each flower has only three petals. The leaves grow in clumps, each on a long stalk. They are broad and oval. The flowers are followed by flat disc-like rings of fruits.

Water-plantain family
Up to 1 m above water
Flowers from June to August
Grows in muddy places or shallow water

64

Bogbean

The exotic white flowers of this plant have a tinge of pink and grow in clusters at the end of leafless stalks. Look for the delicate white fringe around the edges of the petals. The leaves each have three broad leaflets and grow on separate stalks from an underground stem in the mud.

Bogbean family
Up to 30 cm tall
Flowers from May to June
Grows on edges of lakes and ponds, in marshes and fens, also in garden ponds

Arrowhead

Look for whorls of white flowers with purple centres. The male flowers grow at the top of the stem, the female flowers lower down. They give way to dark seed heads. The dark green leaves give the plant its name, being shaped like arrowheads. They grow on long stalks from underground tubers. If you can, look beneath the water to see the long, narrow, translucent, underwater leaves too.

Water-plantain family
Up to 90 cm above water
Flowers from July to August
Grows in shallow water

Frogbit

At first glance, this small floating plant looks like a tiny water-lily. Its rounded leaves float on the water, but they grow in floating rosettes connected by long stems with their roots trailing in the water. The small, white flowers have three petals and three sepals. At the end of autumn special buds grow at the ends of the stems. They sink to the bottom of the pond in winter then rise to grow into new plants next spring.

Frogbit family
Flowers from July to September
Grows in water

Monkeyflower

This plant was brought from North America as a garden flower, but now grows in the wild too. The showy yellow flowers grow from the bases of the upper leaves. Look carefully to see that each has two lips with orange spots in the centre. The leaves are rounded and grow in pairs up the upright stems. Look too for the mats of creeping, leafy stems from which the flowering stems grow.

Figwort family
20–50 cm tall
Flowers from July to September
Grows on the banks of streams and ponds and in marshes

Marsh Marigold

You will easily spot this plant with its large, showy yellow flowers which look like large buttercups. Each flower may have up to 8 petal-like sepals and as many as 100 stamens. Their stalks are hollow. The large, dark green leaves are heart shaped and grow in clumps. Notice their toothed edges and long stalks. The plant is also known as Kingcup.

Buttercup family
Up to 60 cm tall
Flowers from March to June
Grows in shallow water and wet places

Yellow Loosestrife

Look for the clusters of yellow flowers growing towards the tops of tall, leafy stems. The leaves are broad and lance shaped; they grow in pairs or whorls of 3–4 leaves. Notice how the flowers grow from the base of the smaller, topmost leaves. The erect stems grow from creeping, underground stems, or rhizomes.

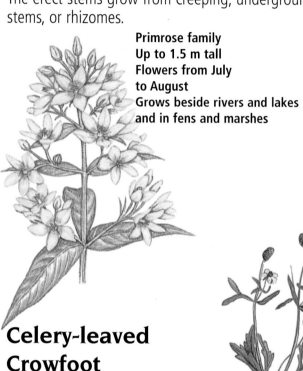

Primrose family
Up to 1.5 m tall
Flowers from July to August
Grows beside rivers and lakes and in fens and marshes

Celery-leaved Crowfoot

Be careful not to touch this plant. Its acrid juice could blister your skin. The small, pale yellow flowers grow at the ends of the stems. The leaves are deeply cut and palmate like celery leaves. Notice how narrow the segments get on the leaves near the top of the stem.

Buttercup family
Up to 60 cm tall
Flowers from May to June

Yellow Flag

This plant has beautiful yellow flowers growing in clusters at the tops of the stalks. The flowers open a few at a time. They each have three hanging petals and three smaller upright ones. The leaves are stiff and sword shaped and grow in clumps as high as the flowers. They grow from dense, tangled underground stems, or rhizomes, which are poisonous and dangerous to animals.

Iris family
About 1 m tall
Flowers from May to July
Grows in marshes and beside rivers and ponds

Yellow Water-lily

You cannot miss the bowl-shaped, yellow flower and heart-shaped, floating leaves of this plant. Notice how the stout stalks keep the flowers clear of the water. Each 'bowl' is formed by the yellow sepals. The yellow petals and stamens surround the broad stigma in the centre. The plant is also called Brandy-bottle, perhaps because its flowers smell of alcohol, or because the fruit is bottle shaped.

Water-lily family
Flowers from June to August
Grows in ponds and slow-moving streams

Common Comfrey

You can recognize this plant from its clumps of large, bristly stems and leaves. Notice how the base of the leaf runs down the stem making it look winged. The flowers may be yellowish-white, pinkish or blue. They grow in coiled clusters at the ends of the stems. Common Comfrey has long been used in herbal medicine for healing wounds, sprains and broken bones. It used to be called Knitbone or Boneset.

Forget-me-not family
Up to 120 cm tall
Flowers from May to June
Grows in damp places such as river banks and wet meadows

Nodding Bur-marigold

The flowerheads of this plant usually have yellow centres surrounded by yellow petals, but the flowers of some plants have only the yellow centres. Look for the leafy bracts behind the flowerhead. They are longer than the petals. The flowerheads begin to nod as they age. They give way to spiky fruits, each with four spines to catch in your clothes. The toothed, lance-shaped leaves grow in pairs.

Daisy family
Up to 60 cm tall
Flowers from July to August
Grows beside streams and ponds

Policeman's Helmet

You cannot mistake the large flowers of this plant. They are unusual and look like pinkish-purple helmets. They grow in clusters on long, drooping stalks from the bases of the topmost leaves. The leaves are toothed and oval and grow in pairs or whorls. Look for the pear-shaped fruits that follow the flowers. Touch the fruits when they are ripe and they will explode, flinging out the seeds.

Touch-me-not family
1–2 m tall
Flowers from July to October
Grows along river banks

Brooklime

You can tell this plant from a Forget-me-not because its flowers have white, not yellow, centres, and each flower has only four petals. Look too at the leaves. They are thick and oval shaped with toothed edges. They grow in pairs up the stems. The young shoots of Brooklime can be chopped into salads, like Watercress, to add a bitter flavour.

Figwort family
Up to 60 cm tall
Flowers from May to September
Grows in ponds and streams and other wet places

Bulrush

These tall plants are unmistakable when the long brown fruit spikes have formed. Look for them in autumn and winter. The flowers form earlier in long spikes, the pollen-laden, yellow, male flowers at the top of the stem and the greenish female flowers below. Look at the leaves too. They are long and sword shaped and grow from the base of the stem in overlapping rows.

Bulrush family
Up to 2.4 m tall
Flowers from June to July
Grows in shallow water over mud

Hemp Agrimony

You cannot miss the reddish-purple flowers of this plant. They form large, flat-topped flowerheads. The flowers are tubular but their white styles make them look fluffy. The leaves grow in pairs up the upright, reddish stem. They are divided palmately into toothed, lance-shaped leaflets. The plant was used a lot at one time as a medicinal herb. It is still useful for treating colds and 'flu.

Daisy family
Up to 120 cm tall
Flowers from June to July
Grows in damp and wet places

Purple Loosestrife

You will easily spot large clumps of this plant with its bright reddish-purple flowers. Look closely at the flower spikes and you will see that they are made up of whorls of many flowers, each with 6 crumpled petals.

Each whorl grows at the base of a pair of whorl of leaves. The leaves are untoothed and lance shaped. Notice that they have no stalks.

Loosestrife family
60–120 cm tall
Flowers from July to August
Grows beside streams and lakes and in marshes

Water Forget-me-not

You will easily recognize these bright blue flowers as Forget-me-nots, with their five blue petals and yellow centres. Notice how the flower cluster is coiled at first, gradually unfurling as the flowers open. The leaves are oval shaped and the stem is hairy. The base of the stem creeps a little then puts down new roots from a rosette of leaves.

Forget-me-not family
Up to 60 cm tall at most
Flowers from May to August
Grows in wet meadows and marshes, and beside streams and ponds

Water Mint

Look for the thick clusters of lilac flowers growing at the bases of the upper leaves and at the top of the stem. Sometimes the clusters are so close they look like one oblong flowerhead. The leaves are oval and toothed. They grow in pairs and smell strongly of spearmint.

Mint family
Up to 90 cm tall
Flowers from July to September
Grows in damp and wet places, like marshes, fens and beside streams and ponds

Great Hairy Willowherb

This plant belongs to the same family as Rosebay Willowherb (see page 19) and looks a bit like it. It forms large patches of upright stems, but its large pinkish-purple flowers grow in clusters, rather than in long spikes. The leaves are lance shaped and covered in soft hairs. The flowers are followed by long pods of silky-haired seeds.

Willowherb family
Up to 1.5 m tall
Flowers from July to August
Grows in marshes and on the edges of ponds and rivers

Things to Make

A flower calendar

You can make a flower calendar to put on your bedroom wall.

1 **Buy a large sheet of paper from an art supply shop** and divide it up into twelve equal areas or strips. Write the name of the months in the centre of the strips.

2 **When you go for a walk**, make a note and a sketch of the flowers you see. If you have a camera you could take a picture instead.

3 **Stick the photo or drawing on to the calendar** in the month you saw the flower.

4 **Alternatively you could copy the picture** of the flower from this book and colour it in yourself before adding it to your calendar; or cut a picture of the flower out of a nature magazine.

For a more detailed record of the wild flowers you see, use an A4 pad of plain paper. When you see a wild flower, make a sketch of it as shown (right). Write down the date you saw it and the place it was growing. Was it in bud, full flower or in seed?

Use a new page for each kind of flower and leave space to add more notes from future walks. As your notes build up, you can put them in a loose-leaf folder.

Book mark

Tall thin flowers make good book marks. You will need one sheet of clear adhesive-backed plastic.

1 **Cut two pieces of the plastic**, make them a little bigger than you the bookmark.

Peel the backing off one piece and lay it sticky side up on a flat surface.

2 **Lay the pressed flower carefully on the sticky plastic.**

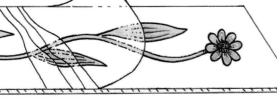

3 **Peel the backing off the other cut piece** and lay it carefully on top of the flower. The two pieces do not need to match up exactly.

4 **Draw the outline of the bookmark on to the plastic** with a biro and cut around the outline through both layers of plastic. The flower will show clearly from both sides of the bookmark.

Flower pictures

You can use dried flowers or pressed flowers (see pages 60–61) to make a picture.

1 **Use a piece of thick paper**, such as cartridge paper or good quality stationery paper. Paint a landscape as a background, if you like.

2 **Arrange the flowers in a pattern** or place them as they would look if they were growing. Do not put the flowers too close to the edge if you are planning to frame your picture.

3 **When you are happy with the arrangement**, stick it down using small amounts of glue on the back of each flower and leaf.

4 **If you have used pressed flowers**, you can frame your picture behind glass. With dried flowers you will have to leave them uncovered.

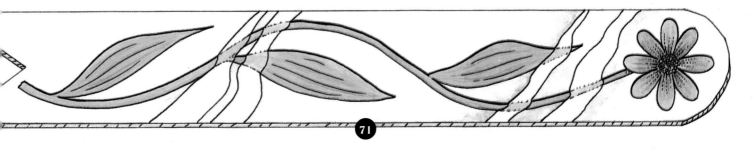

Seaside

Coastal habitats include sand dunes, shingle banks, salt marshes and cliffs. Many plants grow here that will not grow inland, although you will also find many of the hardier inland plants growing on the coast. Coastal plants have to survive harsh winds, salty air and, near to the sea, salty soil too.

In many ways coastal plants are like desert plants. There is so much salt in the air and the soil it is difficult for them to get fresh water. Like desert plants, many have succulent stems and leaves to store water, a tough outer skin to keep the water in, and deep roots.

Be very careful when looking for flowers on marshes, estuaries, narrow beaches and coves; it is all too easy to be cut off by the tide or trapped in soft mud. Never climb up cliffs to look for plants; you will very often find them at the foot of the cliff as well. The picture shows five plants from the book; how many can you recognize?

Sea Beet, Sea Bindweed, Common Stork's-bill, Sea Sandwort, Yellow Horned-poppy

Golden Samphire

It is easy to spot this plant, with its yellow daisy-like flowers and fleshy leaves. The flowers grow in clusters at the ends of the stems. The outer florets are yellow and the centres are a darker orange-yellow. Look closely at the long, narrow leaves. Their tips often have three teeth.

Daisy family
About 60 cm tall
Flowers from July to August
Grows on cliffs, rocks, shingle banks and salt marshes

Yellow Horned-poppy

This plant, with its bright-yellow flowers, is easy to recognize as a poppy. The flowers have four large petals and a thick cluster of stamens in the centre. Look out for the seed pods. They are very long – up to 30 cm – and bend over into the shape of a sickle. The leaves feel rough to touch. They are grey-blue and almost fleshy. Notice how they are divided pinnately into jagged lobes.

Poppy family
30–90 cm tall
Flowers from June to September

Alexanders

This plant has yellow-green flowers which grow in dense clusters at the ends of the stems. The leaves are dark green and shiny. Notice how they clasp the stems. They are divided into three leaflets, which are also divided into three, and then into three again. The lower ones are up to 30 cm long. The stems become hollow and ridged as they age. They were eaten as a vegetable until they were replaced by celery.

Carrot family
Up to 1.5 m tall
Flowers from April to June

Rock Samphire

Look for the stout umbrella-shaped flowerheads of this plant growing at the ends of the many branches of the solid stems. The stem and leaves are blue-grey. The leaves are pinnately divided into narrow fleshy leaflets. The young stems and leaves can be gathered in spring and pickled. The young seed pods can be pickled too.

Carrot family
15–45 cm tall
Flowers from June to August
Grows on cliffs and rocks

Annual Sea-blite

It is hard to spot the flowers on this small sprawling plant. They look like small buttons and grow in clusters from the base of the upper leaves. The leaves are blue-green and fleshy. Annual Sea-blite can be eaten. Add it to soups and casseroles for its salty taste.

Goosefoot family
Up to 30 cm tall
Flowers from July to October
Grows in salt marshes

Sea Plantain

You will easily notice the greenish flower spikes at the end of the long, straight stems. Look for the yellow anthers too. The thick fleshy leaves are long and narrow, and sometimes have toothed edges. They form a rosette at the base of the stalk.

Plantain family
Up to 15 cm tall
Flowers from July to October
Grows in short grass on salt marshes, also by mountain streams

Sea Beet

Look for the reddish, sprawling stems and long spikes of green flowers. Notice how the flowers grow in whorls of three from the base of a small leaf. The flowers give way to brown seeds which stay on the plant for a long time. The leathery leaves are kite shaped and have a reddish tinge. Sea Beet is related to Beetroot and Sugar Beet, but unlike them, it does not have swollen roots.

Goosefoot family
Up to 2 m tall
Flowers from July to September
Grows on shingle beaches, salt marshes and grassy places

Glasswort

This strange-looking plant has upright stems with many jointed branches. The 'joints' are formed by the fleshy leaves. They grow in pairs and are joined along the edge to hug the stem. Young plants are green but turn to yellow, then pink or red as they age. The flowers grow between the segments but are difficult to spot. The plant can be eaten raw in salads or cooked in soups, but do not pick them if they could be polluted.

Goosefoot family
15–30 cm tall
Flowers from August to September
Grows on salt marshes

Sea Sandwort

You will find this plant growing in thick patches from thick stems which run in and along the sand. The many oval leaves are fleshy, so they retain water. Notice how they are arranged in four overlapping ranks. The small white flowers grow from the bases of the upper leaves.

Pink family
Up to 30 cm tall
Flowers from June to August
Grows on beaches and sand dunes

Sea Purslane

This small creeping shrub often forms large colonies. Look for its many silvery leaves fringing the pools in salt marshes. They are thick and fleshy so they do not dry out in the constant sea winds. The thick spikes of yellow flowers grow at the ends of the stems. They are followed by knobbly yellow fruits.

Goosefoot family
Up to 80 cm tall
Flowers from July to September
Grows near the high tide mark, around estuaries and on salt marshes

Seaside

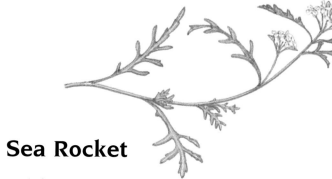

Sea Bindweed

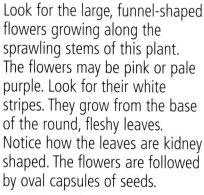

Look for the large, funnel-shaped flowers growing along the sprawling stems of this plant. The flowers may be pink or pale purple. Look for their white stripes. They grow from the base of the round, fleshy leaves. Notice how the leaves are kidney shaped. The flowers are followed by oval capsules of seeds.

Bindweed family
Stems about 60 cm long
Flowers from June to August
Grows on seashores,
sand-dunes and
shingle

Sea Rocket

Look for this sprawling plant just above the high-tide line at the top of the beach. The purple flowers each have four petals and grow in clusters at the ends of the stems. They are followed by stubby fruits which float and spread on the tide. Notice how fleshy the greyish leaves are.

Mustard family
Up to 30 cm tall
Flowers from June to August
Grows on shingle and sandy beaches

Common Scurvy-grass

This plant has long spikes of white flowers growing at the ends of the branching stem. Look for the rosette of fleshy, heart-shaped leaves at the bottom of the stem. These leaves have long stalks, but those higher up the stem have no stalks at all. The leaves are rich in Vitamin C and used to be made into a bitter-tasting tonic taken by sailors on long sea trips. They drank it to prevent the skin disease, scurvy.

Mustard family
Up to 60 cm tall
Flowers from June to August
Grows on cliffs, shingle
and salt marshes

Sea Milkwort

The tiny white or pink flowers of this plant have no petals. The sepals look like petals and form a bell shape. Notice how they grow from the base of the pairs of blue-green, oval leaves. The stems creep along the ground, putting down roots from time to time.

Primrose family
Up to 30 cm tall
Flowers from June
to August
Grows on cliffs and
grassy salt marshes

76

Seakale

This plant produces broad clusters of small, white flowers. Each flower has four petals. The blue-green leaves form large clumps that can easily avoid being buried in the shifting sand and shingle. The leaves are thick and fleshy, with ragged wavy edges. The young shoots can be cooked and eaten like asparagus.

Mustard family
40–60 cm tall
Flowers from June to August
Grows on shingle and sandy shores and on cliffs

Thrift

The tufts of narrow, grass-like leaves of this plant are hard to miss, especially when the dense pink flowerheads are present. They have a sweet scent and are popular with bees. Look for the papery bracts enclosing the flowers, and the bare stems that they grow on. Look beneath the leaves to see the woody stem from which they grow. The plant is also known as the Sea Pink.

Sea Lavender family
Up to 15 cm tall
Flowers from May to July
Grows on cliffs and salt marshes.

Burnet Rose

This rose has stiff bristles on its stems as well as the usual straight prickles. The flowers are creamy-white with five notched petals. They grow on their own at the ends of the stems. Count the number of toothed leaflets on each pinnate leaf – there will be 7 – 11 of them. The flowers are followed by small, round hips, which turn purplish-black when ripe.

Rose family
Up to 60 cm tall
Flowers from May to July
Grows in dry, open places such as sand dunes

Common Stork's-bill

Look for the pink flowers of this plant growing at the ends of sprawling stems. The ferny leaves are pinnately divided into leaflets. The plant gets its name from the fruits, which look like the beaks of storks. When the seeds are ripe, the fruits split into spiralled sections like corkscrews. They screw themselves into the ground so the seed is planted at exactly the right depth.

Geranium family
Stems up to 30 cm long
Flowers from June to September
Grows on old sand dunes and in dry, grassy places

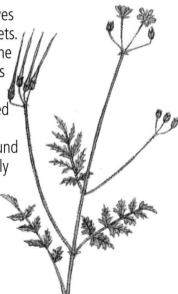

Find Out Some More

Useful organizations

The best organization for you to get in touch with is your local County Wildlife Trust. There are forty-seven of these trusts in Great Britain and you should contact them if you want to know about wildlife and nature reserves in your area. Ask your local library for their address, or contact:

The Wildlife Trusts, The Kiln, Waterside, Mather Road, Newark, Nottinghamshire NG24 1WT (0870 036 7711).

Wildlife Watch is the junior branch of The Wildlife Trusts. Local Wildlife Watch groups run meetings all over the country. Again you can find out about your nearest Wildlife Watch group by contacting The Wildlife Trusts.

Plantlife, 14 Rollestone Street, Salisbury, Wiltshire SP1 1DX (01722 342730). Founded in 1989, they campaign for the conservation of plants and their habitats. Join their campaign to grow Bluebells for Britain.

Field Studies Council, Central Services, Preston Montford, Montford Bridge, Shrewsbury, Shropshire SY4 1HW (01743 852 100). They run interesting courses for families at ten Field Centres throughout England and Wales. They also run many courses for school groups; ask your teacher about these.

In Scotland, contact the **Scottish Field Studies Association**, Kindrogan Field Studies Centre, Enochdhu, Blairgowrie, Perthshire PH10 7PG (01250 870 150).

The Forestry Commission, Public Information Division, 231 Corstorphine Road, Edinburgh EH12 7AT (0131 334 0303). They provide free information sheets about the forests of Great Britain and will tell you how to contact your local branch of the Forestry Commission office, who publish local trail leaflets. There is sometimes a charge for these leaflets.

National Trust for Places of Historic Interest or Natural Beauty, 32 Queen's Anne's Gate, London SW1H 9AB (01793 817400). For membership enquiries: The National Trust Box 39, Warrington WA5 7WD (0870 4584000). They own more than 232,000 hectares of countryside throughout England, Wales and Northern Ireland. These include many woods, nature reserves and sites of special scientific interest. Most are open to visitors, but you may have to pay to get in. The National Trust also run courses with school groups; ask your teacher to find out about these.

In Scotland, contact the Head of Education, **The National Trust for Scotland**, Wemyss House, 28 Charlotte Square, Edinburgh EH2 4ET (0131 243 9300).

Places to visit

You will find wild plants growing wherever you go, even in the middle of a big city. Small woods, hedges and roadsides are good places to look for many of the common species. However, you will find a much wider variety if you visit a classic area for plant spotting. Some of these are listed here:

Roadsides and Hedges: much of southern Pembrokeshire; the West Country;

Woodlands: Forest of Dean, Gloucestershire; the Chiltern woods, Buckinghamshire; the Cotswold woods, Gloucestershire; the Lake District, Cumbria;

Meadows and Pastures: the Downs, Sussex, the Mendip Hills;

Rivers, Ponds and Lakes: the Broads and fens of East Anglia, the Levels, Somerset;

Seasides: the Romney Marshes, Kent; Essex; Norfolk; the Gower peninsula, West Glamorgan; the Isle of Anglesey, Wales; the Western and Northern Isles, Scotland.

Index & Glossary

To find the name of a plant in this index, search under its main name. So, to look up Lesser Celandine, look under Celandine, not under Lesser.

A

Agrimony 26

Agrimony, Hemp 68

Alexanders 73

Anemone, Wood 45

annuals Plants that grow from seed, flower, and die all in the same year 4

anthers The bits at the top of the *stamens* that contain pollen 6

Arrowhead 65

Avens, Water 46

Avens, Wood 43

B

Bedstraw, Hedge 30

Beet, Sea 74

biennials Plants that grow from seed their first year and then flower and die in their second year 4

Bindweed, Field 18

Bindweed, Hedge 28

Bindweed, Sea 76

Blackberry 32

Bluebell 46

Bogbean 65

Bryony, Black 29

Bryony, White 29

Brooklime 68

bulb An underground cluster of thick, juicy leaves acting as a food store 36

Bulrush 68

Bur-marigold, Nodding 67

Burdock, Lesser 21

Buttercup, Creeping 27

Buttercup, Meadow 54

C

Campion, Red 47

Campion, White 29

Carrot, Wild 53

Cat's Ear 54

Celandine, Greater 26

Celandine, Lesser 42

Charlock 12

Chickweed, Common 17

Cinquefoil, Creeping 28

Cleavers 40

Clover, Red 57

Clover, White 52

Cocklebur, Rough 11

Coltsfoot 14

Comfrey, Common 67

Cowslip 55

Crane's-bill, Cut-leaved 18

Crane's-bill, Meadow 34

Cress, Hoary 16

Crowfoot, Celery-leaved 66

Cuckoo-flower 56

Cuckoo-pint 40

D

Dandelion 14

Deadnettle, Red 18

Deadnettle, White 31

Dock, Curled 10

Dog's Mercury 41

Dog-violet, Common 47

Dyer's Rocket 13

E

Evening Primrose 13

Eyebright, Common 52

F

Felwort 58

Figwort, Common 41

Flag, Yellow 67

florets The tiny disk or ray flowers packed together to make a complete flowerhead of daisies and related plants 6

Forget-me-not, Field 20

Forget-me-not, Water 69

Foxglove 46

Frogbit 65

Fumitory, common 20

G

Glasswort 75

Goatsbeard 54

Good King Henry 11

Ground Elder 17

Groundsel 15

H

Harebell 58

Hawksbeard, Smooth 14

Hedge-parsley, Upright 32

Helleborine, Broad-leaved 40

Hemlock 53

Herb Robert 33

Hogweed 31

Honeysuckle 29

Horned-poppy, Yellow 73

Horse Radish 30

I

Ivy, Ground 47

K

Knapweed, Lesser 58

Knotgrass 18

L

Lady's Bedstraw 55

Lady's Mantle 52

Lettuce, Prickly 15

Lettuce, Wall 43

Loosestrife, Purple 69

Loosestrife, Yellow 66

M

Mallow, Common 32

Marigold, Marsh 66

Marjoram, Wild 56

Mayweed, Scentless 16

Meadowsweet 63

Melilot, Ribbed 13

Milkwort, Sea 76

Mint, Water 69

Monkeyflower 66

Moschatel 41

Mugwort 33

Mullein, Great 27

Mustard, Garlic 27

Mustard, Hedge 12

Mustard, Treacle 12

N

Nettle, Stinging 10

Nightshade, Enchanter's 45

Nightshade, Woody 34

Nipplewort 15

O

Orache, Common 10

Orchid, Common Spotted 57

Orchid, Early Purple 46

Orchid, Green-winged 59

Orchid, Pyramidal 56

ovary The female part of the flower where the eggs are produced 6, 23

P

Pansy, Field 13

Parsley, Cow 30

Parsley, Fool's 17

Parsley, Garden 14

Parsnip, Wild 26

Pennycress, Field 16

Pepperwort, Field 31

perennials Plants that live for several flowering seasons 4

Pineapple Weed 27

Plantain, Greater 10

Plantain, Sea 74

Index & Glossary

Policeman's Helmet 68

pollen The powder from the *anthers* which fertilizes the eggs in the ovary 6, 22–23

pollination How *pollen* is carried from the *anthers* to the *stigma* 4, 22–23

Poppy, Field 19

Primrose 42

Purslane, Sea 75

R

Radish, Wild 12

Ragged Robin 57

Ragwort, Common 27

Ramsons 44

Restharrow, Common 59

rhizome A thick under-ground stem where plants store food 4

Ribwort 52

Rocket, Sea 76

Rockrose, Common 55

Rose, Burnet 77

Rose, Dog 33

S

Sage, Wood 41

St John's-wort, Common 43

Samphire, Golden 73

Samphire, Rock 73

Sandwort, Sea 75

Sanicle 45

Scabious, Devil's bit 59

Scabious, Field 35

Scarlet Pimpernel 19

Scurvey-grass 76

Sea-bite, Annual 74

Seakale 77

seeds Ripened eggs of a flower 23, 36–7

Self-heal 21

sepals The green leaflike pieces around the base of the flower, which protected the bud 6

Sheep's-bit 35

Shepherd's Purse 17

Silverweed 28

Snowdrop 44

Sorrel, Sheep's 53

Sorrel, Wood 44

Sow-Thistle, Prickly 15

Speedwell, Germander 34

Speedwell, Ivy-leaved 21

Spurge, Sun 11

Spurrey, Corn 16

stamens The male parts of the flower. At the top of them are the *anthers* 6

stigma The female part of the flower, attached to the ovary, that receives pollen 6

Stitchwort, Greater 44

Stork's Bill, Common 77

stomata Tiny holes in the leaves of plants which take in air and let out water and carbon dioxide gas 38

Strawberry, Barren 42

Strawberry, Wild 43

style The tube connecting the *style* with the *ovary*. Pollen travels down the *style* to fertilize the eggs in the ovary 6

T

Teasel 34

Thistle, Creeping 20

Thistle, Musk 59

Thistle, Stemless 58

Thrift 77

Thyme, Wild 56

Toadflax, Common 26

Toadflax, Ivy-leaved 35

Tormentil 54

Traveller's Joy 28

Trefoil, Bird's-foot 55

Twayblade 40

V

Valerian, Red 33

Vetch, Tufted 35

W

Water-crowfoot 64

Water-dropwort 63

Water-lily, White 64

Water-lily, Yellow 67

Water-plantain 64

Watercress 63

Watercress, Fool's 63

wilderness garden 36

Willowherb, Great Hairy 69

Willowherb, Rosebay 19

Woodruff, Sweet 45

Woundwort, Hedge 32

X

xylem Tiny tubes which carry water up from the roots to the leaves of plants 48

Y

Yarrow, 30